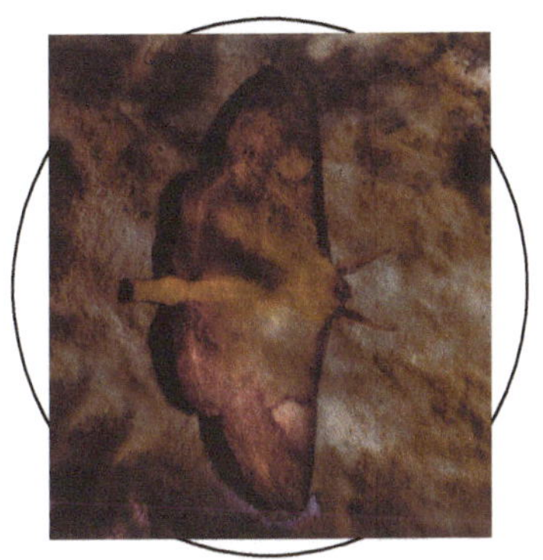

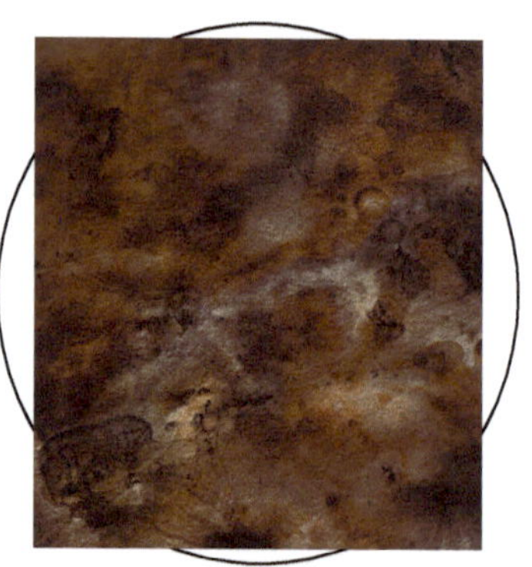

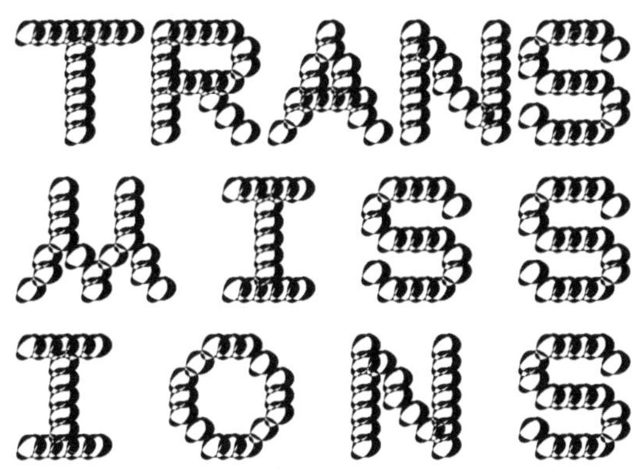

SPECULATIVE FIELD STUDIES AT THE GOONHILLY DOWNS SSSI EARTH STATION

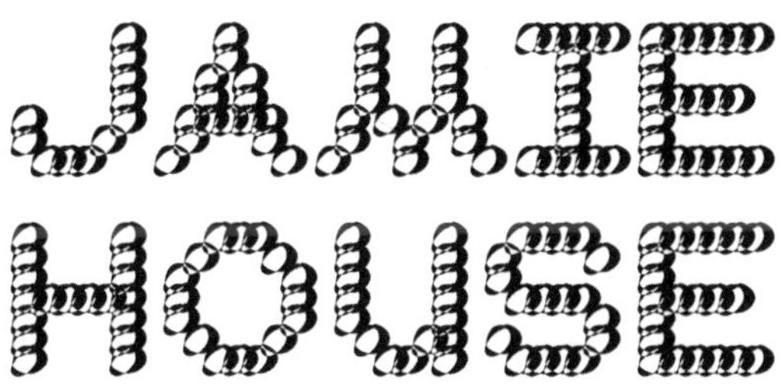

(

) Dedicated to June House &
Katherine Moore   (

) for their selfless love,
encouragement   (

) and support

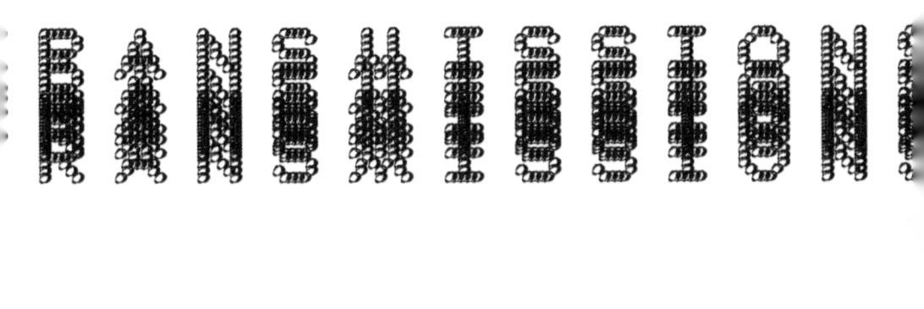

TRANSMISSIONS

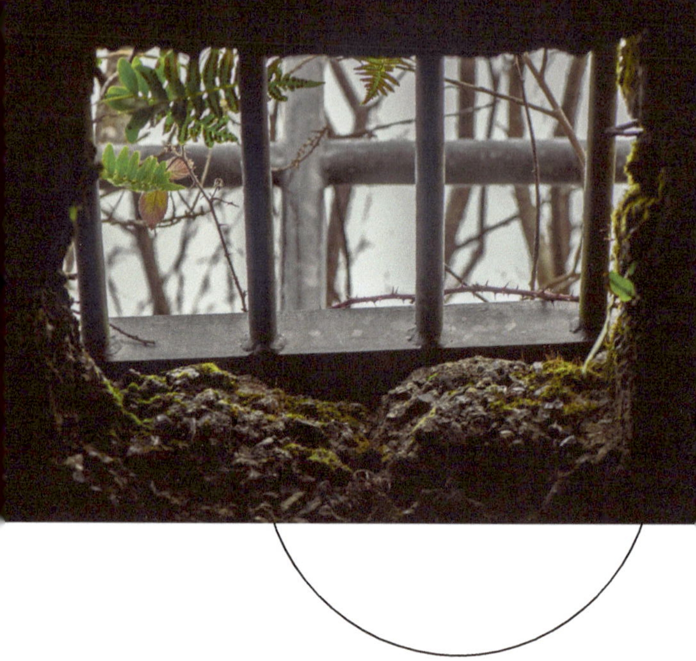

GOONHILLY DOWNS SSSI CORNWALL UK

AREA: 1,271.0 hectares

AZIMUTH: 227.5° (224.7° magnetic)

ELEVATION: 48.7°

LNB SKEW: +41.6°

CURRENT SUN-EARTH-SATELLITE ANGLE: 127°

LATITUDE: 25.7796°

LONGITUDE: 51.2059°

LOCATOR: LL55OS

GEOLOGY: The Lizard Complex has been interpreted as a dismembered ophiolite obducted during the upper Palaeozoic Variscan Orogeny. The complex is constructed of three tectonic units each separated by low-angle faults; the Crousa Downs Unit, Goonhilly Downs Unit, and Basal Unit.

TERRAIN: The site forms the central core of the Lizard heathlands, the largest remnant of a formerly more extensive serpentinite heathland. The site is mainly underlain by serpentinite, with small outcrops of granite gneiss and hornblende schist.

SUBMARINE CABLES: Cables SEA-ME-WE 3, UK-Channel Islands 8.

NOTABLE LANDMARKS: GHY-1 listed satellite. Standing stone dating to the bronze age. Roughly 3m tall, it extends an additional metre below the ground.

(

) The ancestors who placed it upright in the ground 3000 years ago somehow brought it here from Crousa Downs, roughly 2 miles away. This effort indicates not only the possible ritual significance of the site but of this particular stone. The Dry Tree stone is a massive piece of gabbro rock. Originally black in colour, gabbro is a course-grain, magnesium and iron rich igneous rock. It is formed deep in the earth by the slow cooling of magma.

NOCTURNAL FIELD STUDIES

(INVESTIGATING THE GOONHILLY DOWNS SSSI EARTH STATION)

Viburnum opulus, Erica vagans, Molinia caerulea,
Pyrus mallus, Pisonia aculeata L, Prunus spinosa L.

VHF, UHF, L, S, C, X, Ku, Ka.

This is a taxonomy of the red data book of threatened plant species at Goonhilly Downs biogenetic
nature reserve. The frequencies listed are those
emitted and received by the satellites situated at
this site for research. Due to its underlying serpentine geology and elevated position, Goonhilly
has never been a place of permanent habitation but
rather one of study and experimentation.

The narratives recounted are kaleidoscopic, where
past, present and imagined futures merge and over-
lap; from standing stones to satellite dishes, from
plants to planets. The intermingling layers of time
and reality can be envisioned through Deleuze's meta-
phorical reading of "Crystal-images", in which stages
of layered time co-exist in a permeable state.

We can think of the Crystal-image as that which
occupies two states simultaneously; a past liquid
state turning into a solid present; a fluid showing its potential to harden or freeze; a virtual
state turning into actual. The Crystal-image shows
us time at work, a 'time-image'. This time-image

is one infused with time—different-from-itself, virtual-to-itself, infused with past/future tenses.

Deleuze surmises: "What the crystal reveals or makes visible is the hidden ground of time, that is, its differentiation into two flows, that of presents which pass and that of pasts which are preserved. Time simultaneously makes the present past and preserves the past in itself. There are, therefore, already, two possible time-images, one grounded in the past, the other in the present. Each is complex and is valid for time as a whole." (Deleuze, 1989: 98)

My work, like time-images, unfolds non-chronologically, showing the viewer different temporalities captured through the act of photography. The result is the crystalline structure of images that form perception and interpretation. Demonstrating a splitting of time beyond the image's apparent connection to movement—time-images. Free from depicting space and time as interdependent, tense becomes irrelevant to the image, opening us up to the past, present, and futures, the imagined timescales of plants and non-humans.

In photographic terms this could be described as a virtual image crystallising into an actual optical image, a 'simultaneous double' as Deleuze describes (Deleuze, 1989: 68). A Crystal-image is one that's capable of showing us both the virtual and the actual; a mirror image.

Goonhilly thought of in Deleuzian terms reveals several mirror structures linking a number of different orders, including reflections of the monolithic GHY1 satellite's past lives, broadcasting the moon landing across the globe. What was it sensing? What is it sensing now? With what non-human entities is it communicating through its radio waves? These ineffable questions on the fringes of representational language fascinate me—the large edifice which became obsolete decades ago still maintained. We have shared strange moments together at night. I am wondering if its intergalactic sensing capabilities are becoming more than just latent possibilities. Future plans will hopefully secure GHY1's otherworldly legacy through the upgrading of its antenna for radio astronomy. Will GHY1 reach far beyond our solar system? Beyond our human perception? And by so doing, help us to understand more about the formation of the stars, enabling the observation of other galaxies and the exploration of black holes.

From this structure to the prehistoric Dry Tree Menhir which stands next to the Satellite Station, we can see a continuity of duration, a depth of time (not space), where regions of time interlink, an example of what Deleuze describes as a 'deep focus shot' (where objects in the past are seen in the deep background, and present action in the exaggerated foreground). Through this we see temporality as an independent dimension and the 'continuity of duration' (Deleuze, 1989: 108).

There is a strange confluence of time juxtaposing the ancient early bronze age stones and the satellites (themselves surrounded by a number of rare plant species). This stone is a well-preserved ceremonial marker which maps the solar system and shares traditional ecological knowledge. Showing both scientific insight and indigenous understanding, David Suzuki and Peter Knudtson's *Wisdom of the Elders* offers a way (through listening to our elders) to reconcile our place in nature. (Suzuki, 1992)

The antithesis of this is shown in the advanced technology of the satellite looming in the background.

This site encompasses a time beyond anthropocentric capitalism; it is moved by experiential notions of temporality, what Henri Bergson (a progenitor of Deleuze's time-image) would label as 'la duree.' (Bergson, 2004). This is not easily measured in the linear time of hours, weeks, years and so on. Because we know that the quality of our experiences varies so much—a moment can be as significant as a year. Clock time is only a human construct designed to help us act navigate the anthropocene.

Deleuze's notion of the 'peaks of the present' follows the crystal as a means of showing us present, past and future. For Bergson, the actual present is an elusive moment between past and future, making it hard to get a stable notion of. In practice we operate with different senses of the present—not so much the actual moment, but a present of the past and of futures to come. This experience offers a portal to see beyond chronological time and the supposed importance of the actual present moment. Instead, we can think of a 'peak present', (Deleuze 1989) one which informs us particularly about the temporality of objects, offering a useful perspective of events. We can activate the chronological past of an event and bring it into the present, adding together past and present characteristics to develop a clear point of view.

There are other implications, although outside of Deleuze's discussion of duration: that of the non-human, living and inanimate. Those that do not have memories of experience, but that are similarly occupying a particular interval in time or duration, which has given them particular characteristics and qualities that show indexes or data of time.

These ancient narratives are embedded in the serpentine stone strata of Goonhilly—in my work composed, revised, forgotten, and re-discovered. Author Jeffrey Cohen explores a "human-lithic-world participation that gathers millennia, layered and deep, opening to expansive historical scales, material insistence, environmental embroilment, densely sedimented temporalities, a community of peoples, things, and forces en-meshed through story and stone." (Cohen, 2015: 77).

He discusses geological and non-human time: "lithic architectures and other nonverbal petroglyphs (including the fossilized remains of various life forms) can communicate across obliterating sweeps of time; and tracing the temporal knot formed when distant history touches present story, since to narrate the past conjures possible futures." (Cohen, 2015: 78).

The time and activity of entangled multispecies embedded in this landscape could as well be situated within Joanna Zylinska's figuration of "nonhuman photography" where she suggests turning phenomena such as fossilisation into an image process.

She muses: "Considering the history of photography as part of the broader nature-cultural history of our planet, I trace parallels between photographs and fossils, and propose to understand photography as a light-induced process of fossilization occurring across different media. Photography thus can be said to bear a material record of life rather than just its memory trace. But I also turn to photography's original reliance on the natural light emanating from the sun to explore what photographic practice can tell us about energy sources, and about our relation to the star that nourishes our planet." (Zylinska, J 2017: 10).

A philosophical account of duration is expansive from the lithosphere to the hydrosphere. From plants to the dead planets the satellites are sending their signals to. In Deleuzian terms, duration is a multiplicity, a cluster of related but diverse possibilities. Some are realised, while others remain virtual or potential. I feel that each nocturnal encounter has a different focus; from the sonic vibrational worlds to those beyond human perception. Electromagnetic microphones present potentialities, offering ways of navigating the site and the world through more-than-human perspectives. But everything is changing through time, even something as apparently solid as a standing stone is slowly and continually being eroded by the harsh Cornish environment.

How do we measure this? How is it shown? We need a type of time that displaces the human, disintegrating those hierarchies and allowing other worlds of possibilities: a realm of deep time.

Deep time opens us to the concept of landscape formation (Allen, 2016). A sense of geologic time allows those creating these histories to understand the scope of the content, and realistically interpret the timescale and involved processes. Imagining millions of years of firsts; geological strata forming through chemical processes, the slow crystallisation of minerals in the ancient oceans forming rock. From water, single-celled life, photosynthesis, Eukaryotes, multicellular life, anthropoid's molluscs, dinosaurs, mammals, plants, flowers, birds and primates.

Photography provides us with an enhanced perception of the confluence of past, present and future imaginings, allowing us to pursue the autonomous and non-hierarchical time not grasped in subjective understandings. Grasping the fragments of the past and then linking them together through photography challenges linear forms of narrative.

Theorist Duncan Wolldridge explores this temporality as it persists within the still image, unraveling traditional notions of time. He suggests that the photograph reveals and informs both past and future simultaneously. Wooldridge re-thinks the entrenched theory of Barthes with its eidos of the photograph as death and the "that has been" past tense, re-activating it into a future tense aligned to a world to come, rather than a world that has been. (Wooldridge, 2021).

Wooldridge considers Marine Hugonnier's expeditionary images captured on the Bering Strait, looking across from Alaska to Russia in one of the few places where the earth's curvature can be clearly perceived. This is a site of dramatic rupture, where one day encounters the next. As Huggonnier looks across the International Date Line she stands at one end of time, and reaches towards its other extreme. She is seeing tomorrow. These images dismantle the authority of temporality. Other times rush in, invade our consciousness, inform our sense of temporality and place. Time here is multi-dimensional, the past not excluding the future, and the future not limiting the past. Hugonnier has de-constructed, an exploded diagram opening up time's complexity, showing how linear time can be modified and transformed. (Wooldbridge, 2021: 155)

I aim to challenge these linear understandings of clock and calendar time as a means to open up new possibilities in the entanglement of deep and photographic time. The crystal-image encompasses these two aspects: the internal limit of all relative circuits, but also the outer-most. The little crystalline seed and the vast crystallisable universe: everything is included, everything has the capacity to expand, as constituted by the seed and the universe.

My field studies are not fixed, and as the photograph is a series of becomings, arriving not fully-formed, continuing to change, remaining unstable. Kaja Silverman discusses the medium as encasing an "unstoppable development", its slippery resistance to being fixed at the time of its early inventions and innovations. (Wooldridge, 2021: 61)

I try to allow the Downs to express itself through a practice of nocturnal wanderings, carried out sonically and virtually on the edges of human perception. A dérive that's sympathetic to plants and which leads to experiential knowings of how to circumnavigate the site from multifaceted human and more-than-human perspectives.

This essay was adapted from a paper delivered at *Phytogenesis II Provocations of Plants, Philosophy and Photography.* **International Symposium University of Plymouth, North East Photography collective, Newcastle University 2022. (**

) **BIBLIOGRAPHY**

Allen, P (2008). *Time scales of tectonic landscapes and their sediment routing systems* Imperial College London.

Badiou, A. (2000). *Deleuze. The clamor of Being.* Minneapolis: University of Minnesota Press.

Bergson, H. (2004) [1912] *Matter and Memory.* New York: Dover Publications.

Bogue, R. (2003) *Deleuze on Cinema.* London: Routledge.

Deleuze, G (1989) *Cinema 2 -- the time-image,* London the Athlone Press.

Deleuze G and Guattari F (2004) [1987] A *Thousand Plateaus,* London: Continuum.

Deleuze, G.and Guattari, F. (2012) *Kafka. Toward a Minor Literature.* Trans. Dana Polan. Minneapolis: University of Minnesota Press.

Wooldridge, W (2021) *To be determined* SPBH publishing.

Cohen, J J. (2015) *Stone An ecology of the inhuman.* University of Minnesota Press Minneapolis.

Zylinska, J (2017) *Nonhuman Photography.* MIT Press.

Suzuki, D (1992) *Wisdom of the Elders.* Bantam Publishing.

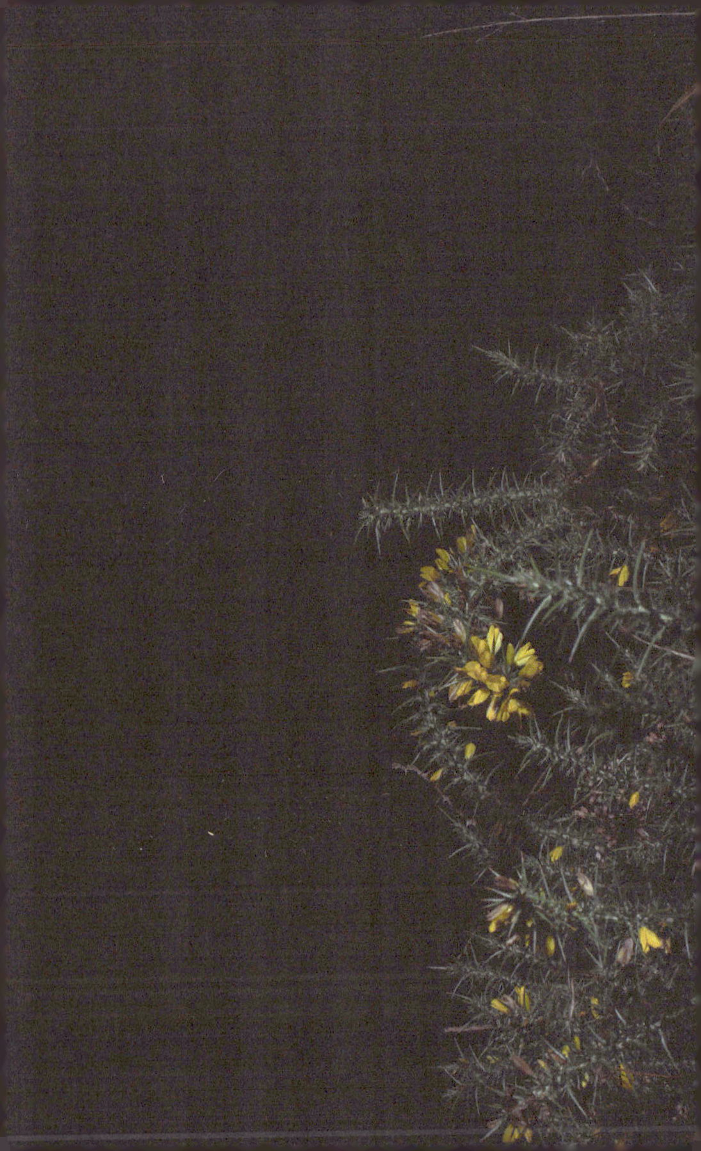

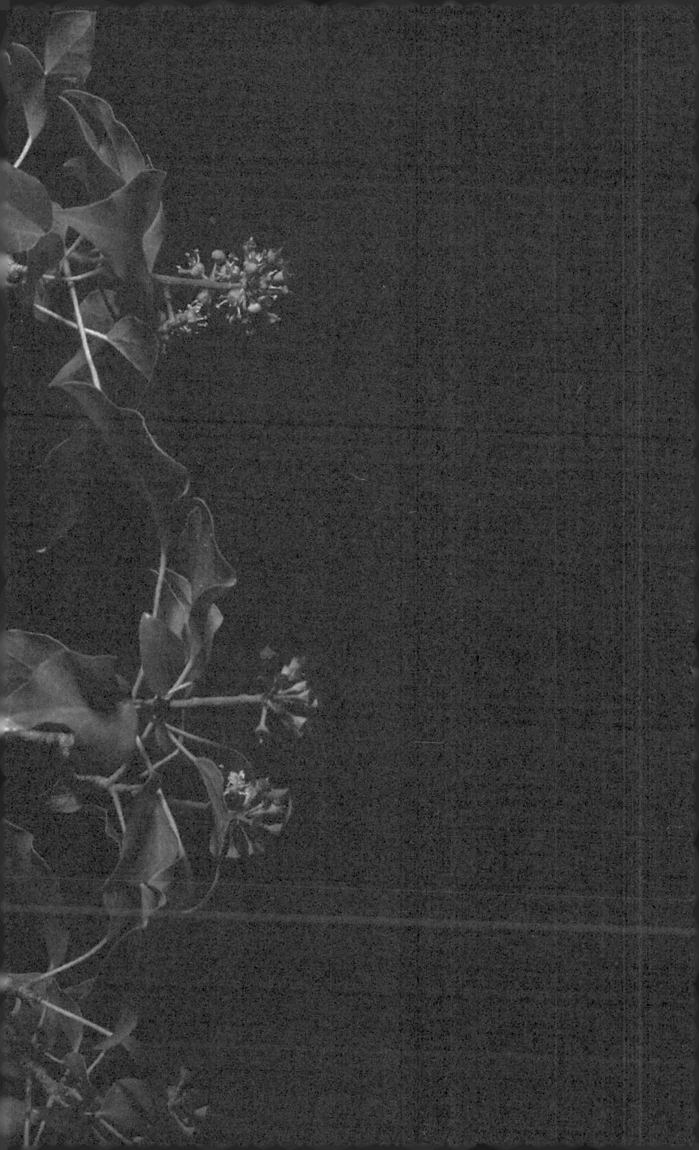

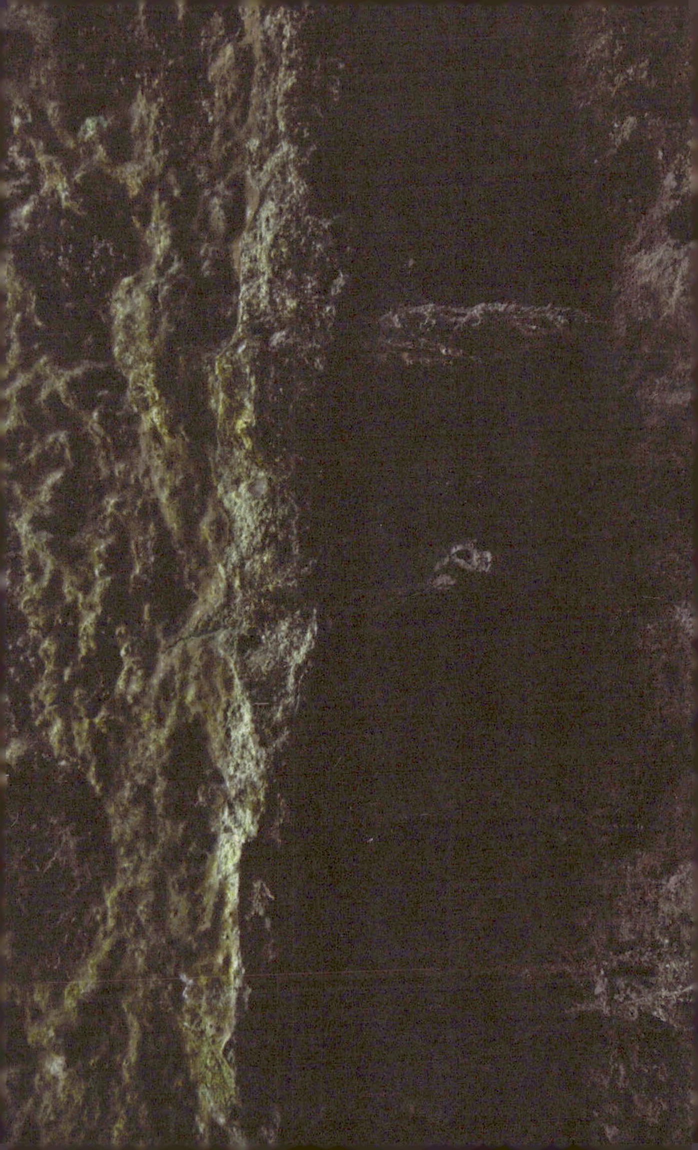

SPECULATIVE FIELD STUDY

Observing life cycles beyond my comprehension.

The antenna reach as branches into the sky, detecting light and gravity, communicating with the cosmic dust.

I am intermittently plunged into terrestrial darkness, relishing the pauses between the satellite's luminous intervals. I am immersed in the nocturnal sonic landscape, its flux, its duree.

An image of the night sky compresses the space-time continuum trillions of kilometres onto its flat plane like a botanical sample pressed onto cardstock.

The black void punctured by a sea of celestial bodies.

As you gaze into more distant objects, the effect is multiplied. The stars of the Big Dipper range from sixty to one hundred and twenty five light-years away. When you look at Dubhe, the front star in the "bowl" of the Dipper, you are seeing light from before you were born—time compressed profoundly into a single image.

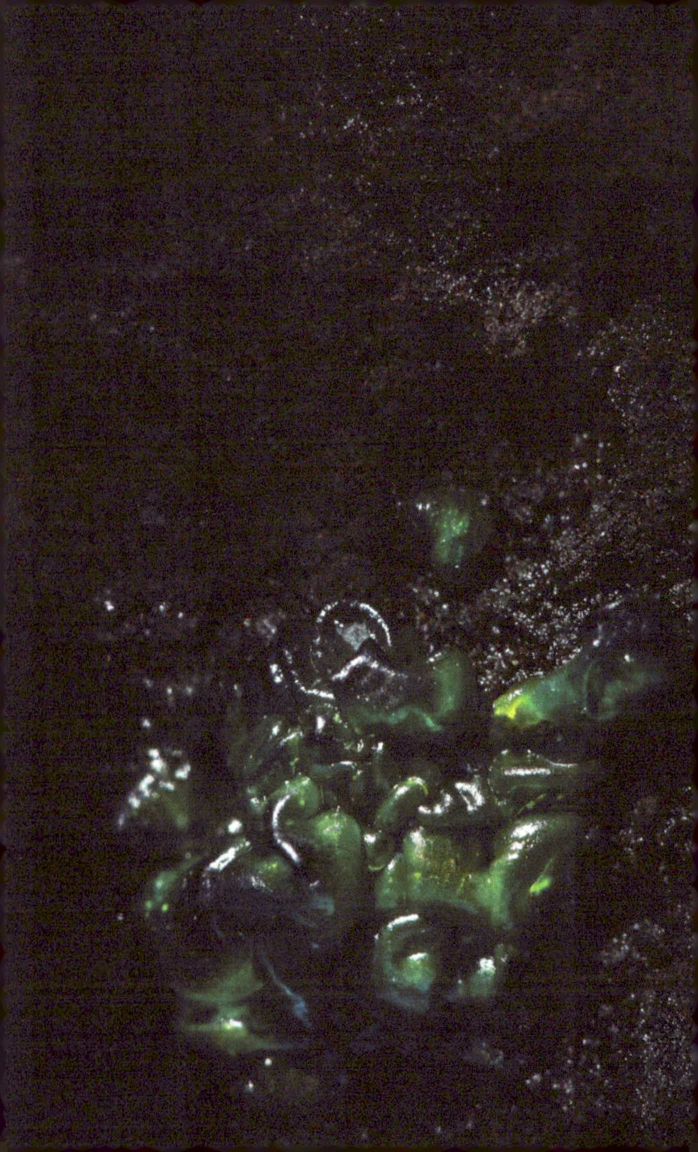

SPECULATIVE FIELD STUDY
(OBJECTS, ARTIFACTS AND SAMPLES)

Attuning (sensing) to the wetlands, strata and deep space communications.

The mud, how acidic is it? What conditions does it produce to cultivate the rare red data book species that live here?

Checking depths of soil horizons.

Sampling and identifying rocks.

Sampling plants.

Leaving reactive art materials in situ.

Making textured stone rubbings on perma trace paper.

Recording the sounds of the earth's magneto-sphere and vibrational forces using geophones and VLF radio scanners.

Methods of photo-material entanglement with the site enfolds various organic matter, such as moss, lichen, fungi, mud and bog water into the image as a means of production.

Working alongside the frequencies in the ether.

This is an ongoing art practice that attempts
to disclose the shifting rhythms of human
and non-human assemblages taking place at a
moment of environmental change and climate
crisis within such a fragile space.

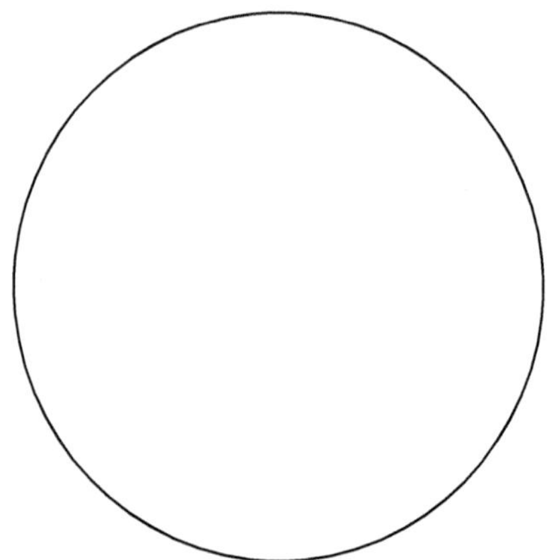

Using multi-disciplined methodologies from
tentacular listening (Haraway) to Para-photo-mancy
(Karel Doing); producing work not made through
purely scientific or photographic means, but
through the material, expressive and creative
quality of the environment itself. An entangled
image-making and sonic process that attunes the
primal poetics of matter.

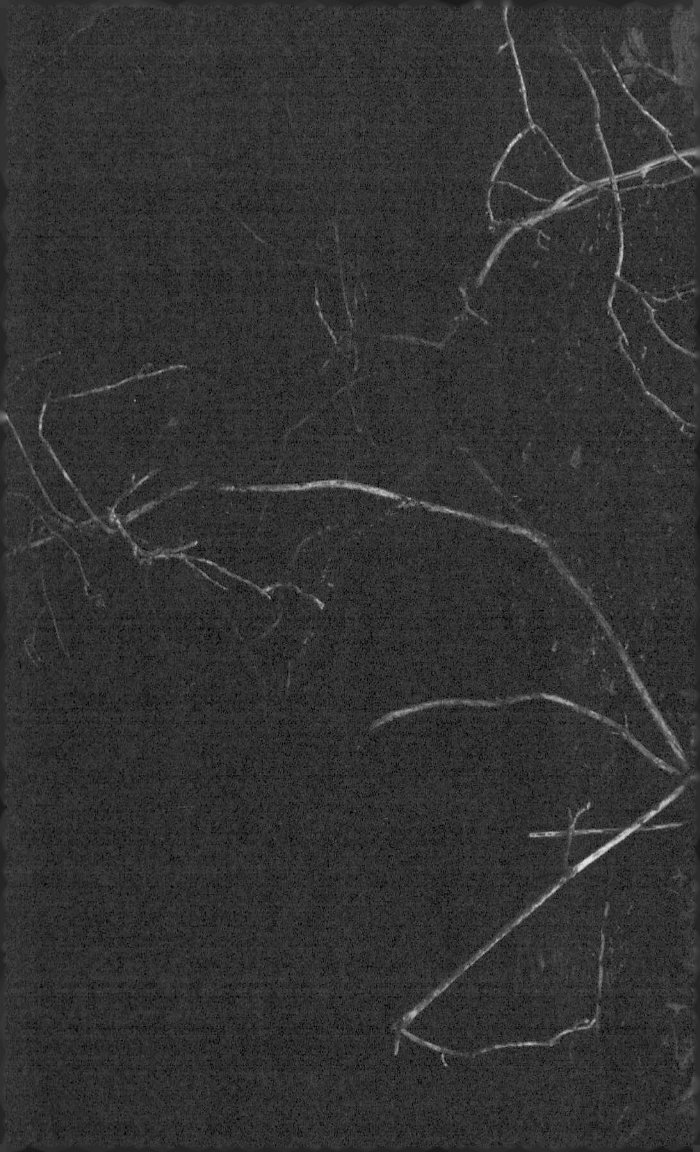

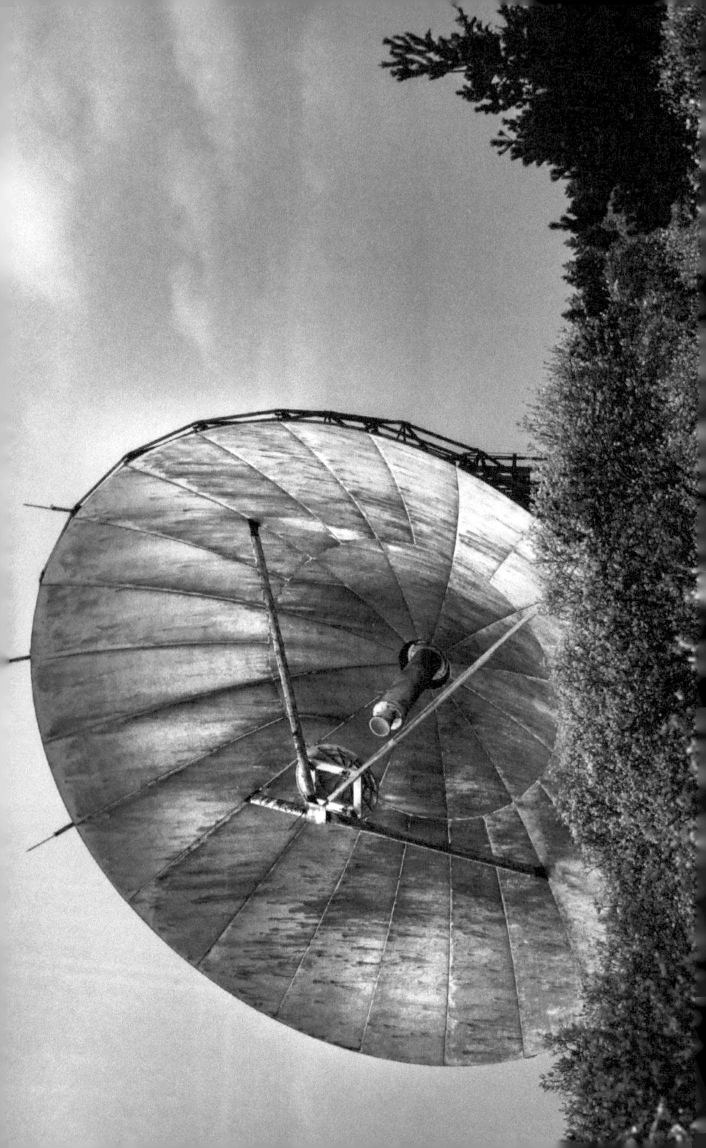

Goonhilly Downs is famed for its heathland habitat. It supports a diversity of plant species including Cornish Heath, Purple Moor Grass, sedges, mosses, butterworts and orchids. Species found here are found nowhere else in the world.

(

) Goonhilly Downs is archaeologically
significant for its large concentration of Early
Bronze Age (c2500 to 1500 BC) round barrows. The
Dry Tree menhir (standing stone) forms part of
a well-preserved ancient ceremonial landscape at
Dry Tree, the highest point of the Downs. The
standing stone, which had been toppled in antiq-
uity, was only re-erected in 1928. There is also
a large barrow, named in an Anglo-Saxon charter
as cruc drænoc or 'barrow at thorns', which marks
the meeting point of five parish boundaries, and
is also a waymark along an important medieval
trackway.

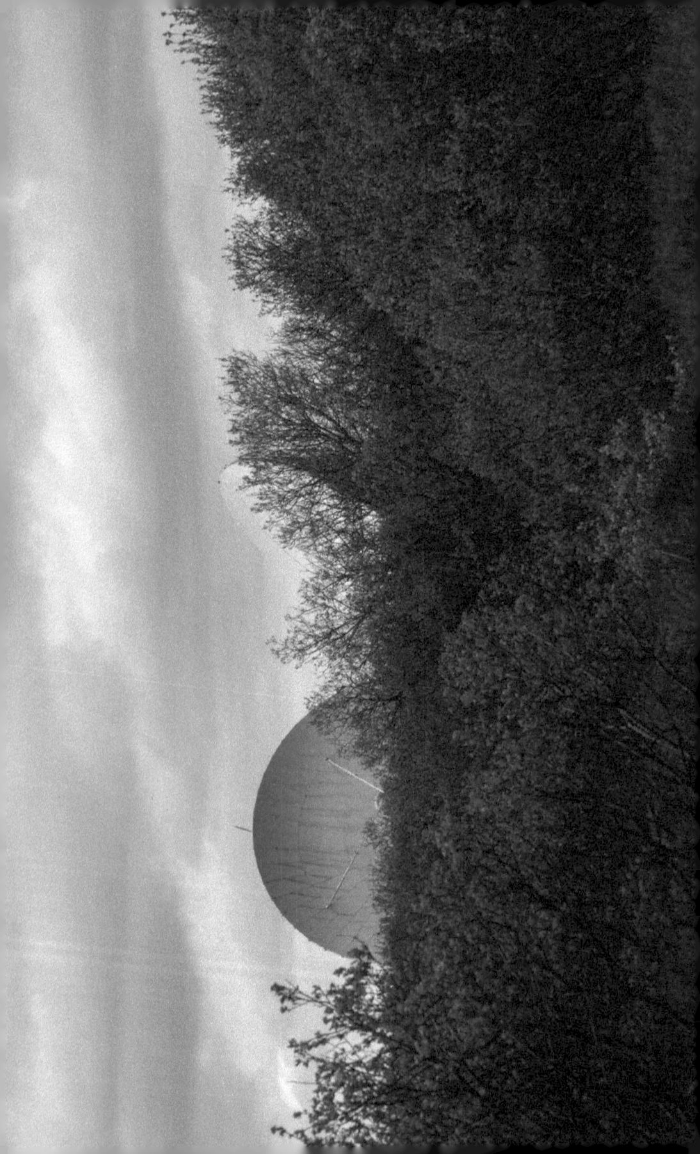

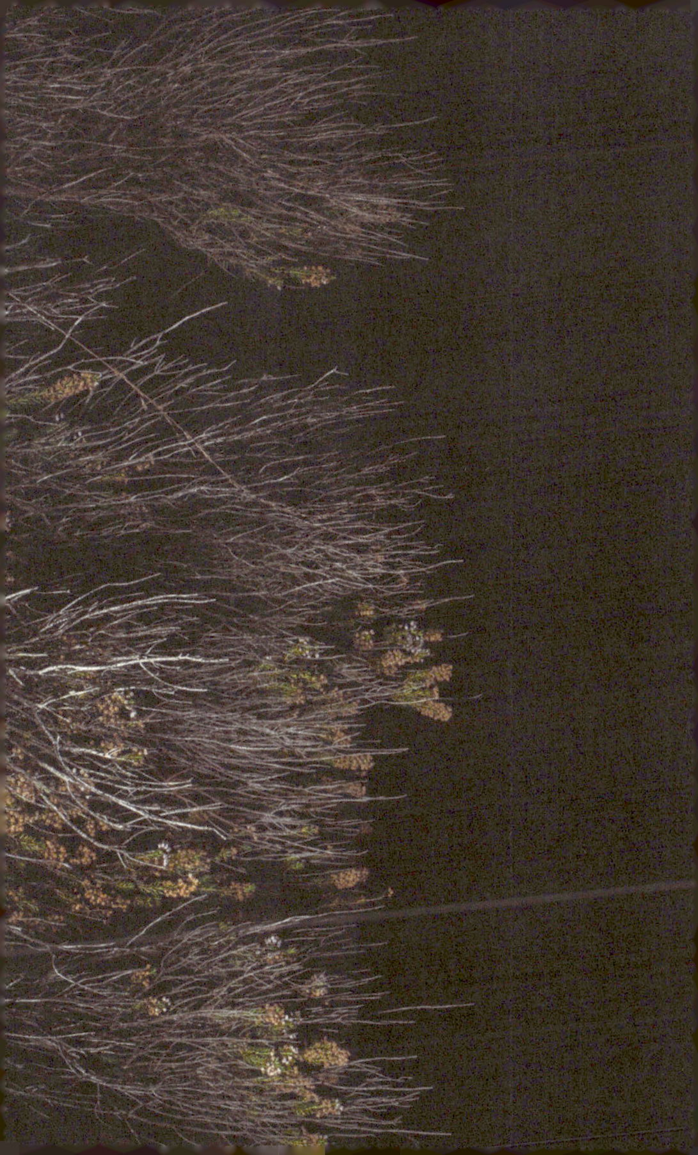

(

) The Earth Station is built on part of the site of a WW2 Chain Home radar station, RAF Dry Tree, and the concrete bases of the radar receiver, transmitter masts, and mast stays are scattered throughout the site, as well as the remnants of over fifty buildings and more than one hundred anti-landing obstructions. The nearby area housed another three radar bases (Treleaver, Trelanvean and Pen Olver) and an airfield at RAF Predannack. The 'Happidrome' was a nickname for a specific type of radar building. It was located at RAF Treleaver, not on the Dry Tree site. The building was named after a popular BBC radio series of the era.

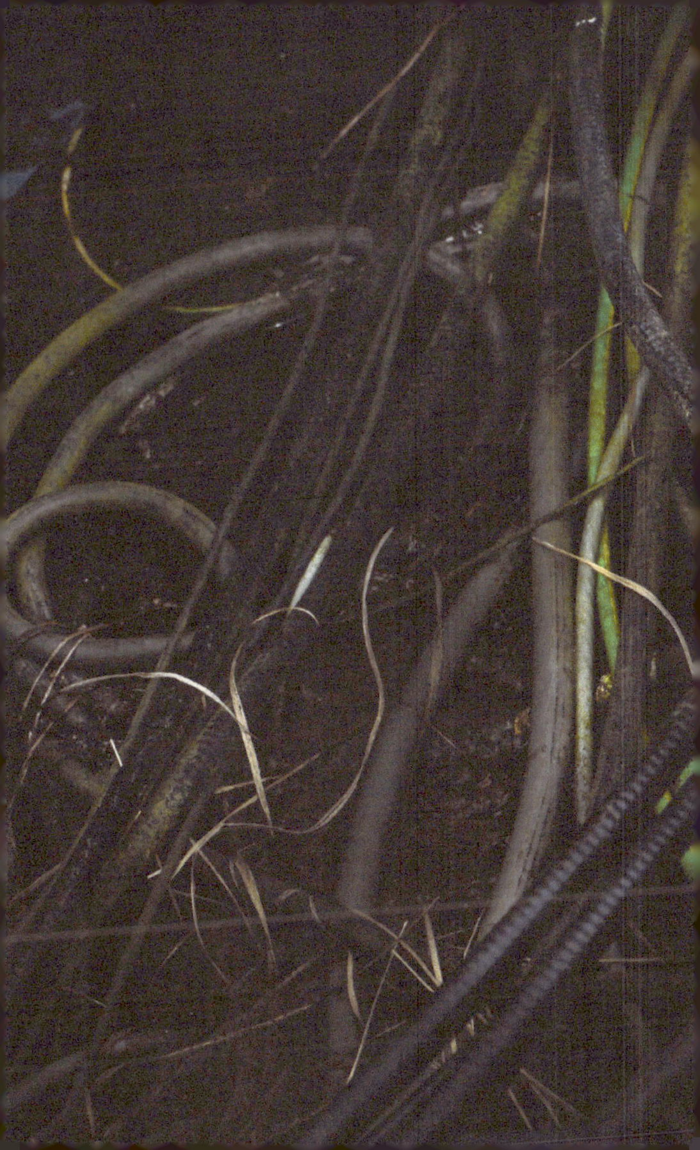

(

　　) It has been sixty-three years since the launch of the Telstar satellite, an emblem of human-driven progress, and the globally televised performance of authority in JFK's accompanying press conference.

This early moment of techno-media convergence, transmitted from the U.S. to Europe via Goonhilly Earth Station's massive Aerial-1 ('Arthur'), and the French Plemeur Bodou station, signified not just human achievement but the beginning of an expanding machinic network that would reshape planetary connectivity.

Telstar has now been discarded, and replaced by more advanced, complex systems. Yet Goonhilly Aerial-1, the 1100-tonne colossus, persists as a relic of shifting temporalities standing ready to evolve again as part of a distributed, multiscalar network of antennas attuned to the cosmic and post-terrestrial flows of radio astronomy. In this new phase, the human figure fades further from the centre, as what were once tools become agents in their own right within an ever-expanding, intelligent ecosystem.

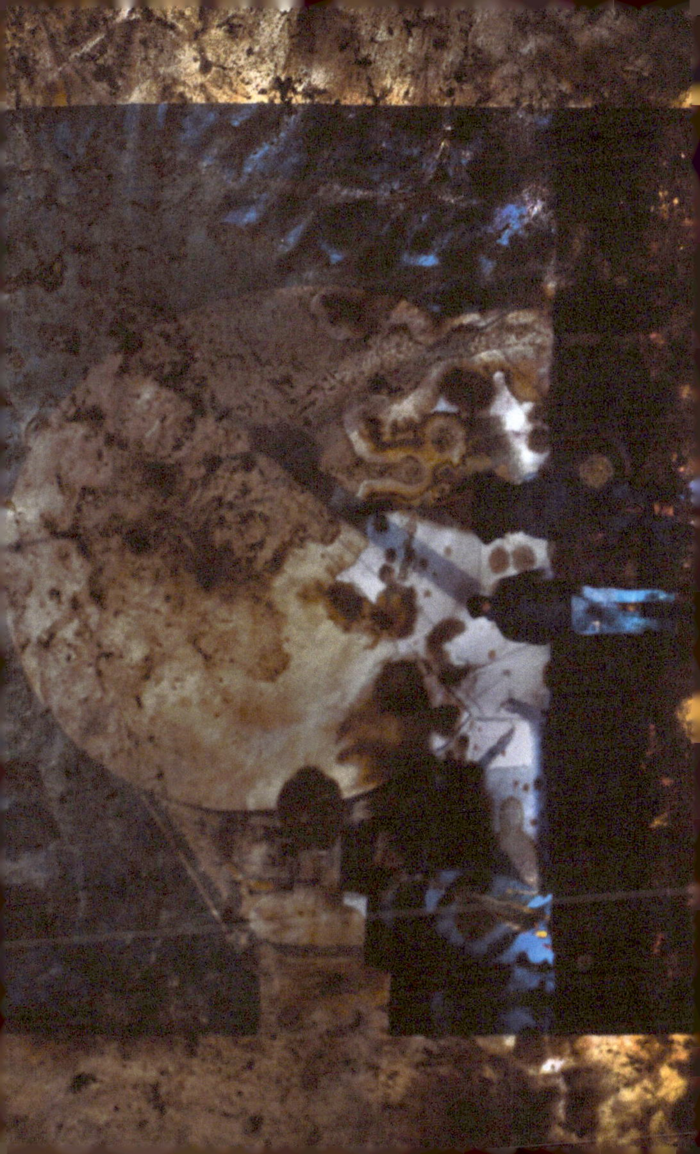

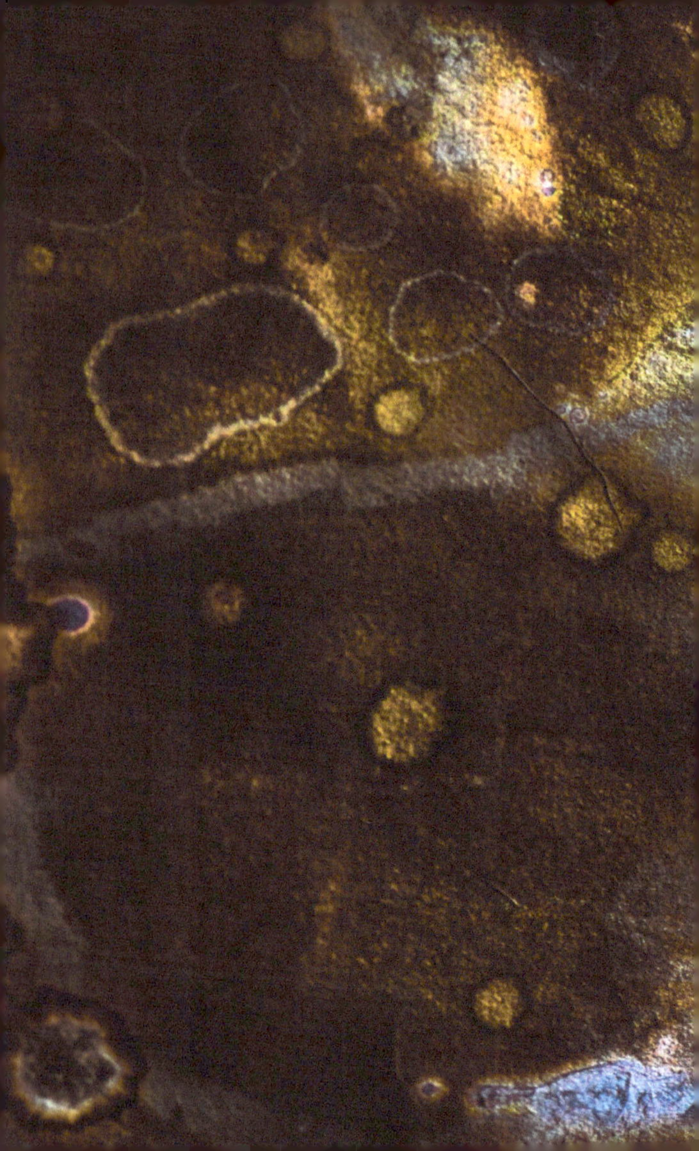

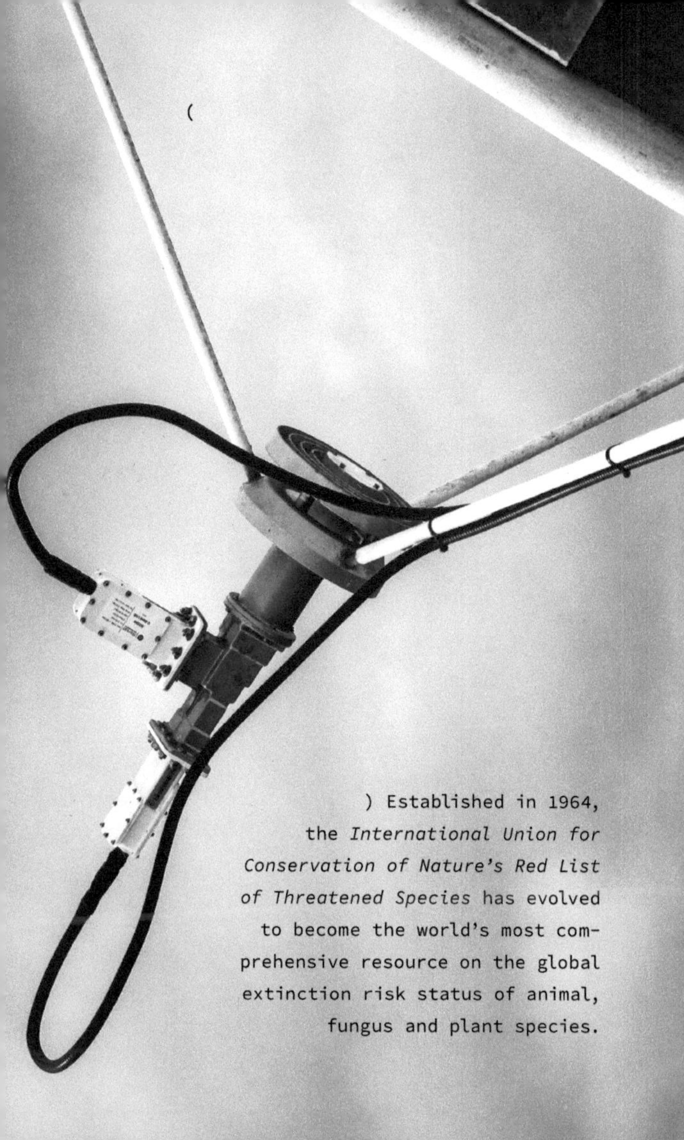

(

) Established in 1964,
the *International Union for
Conservation of Nature's Red List
of Threatened Species* has evolved
to become the world's most com-
prehensive resource on the global
extinction risk status of animal,
fungus and plant species.

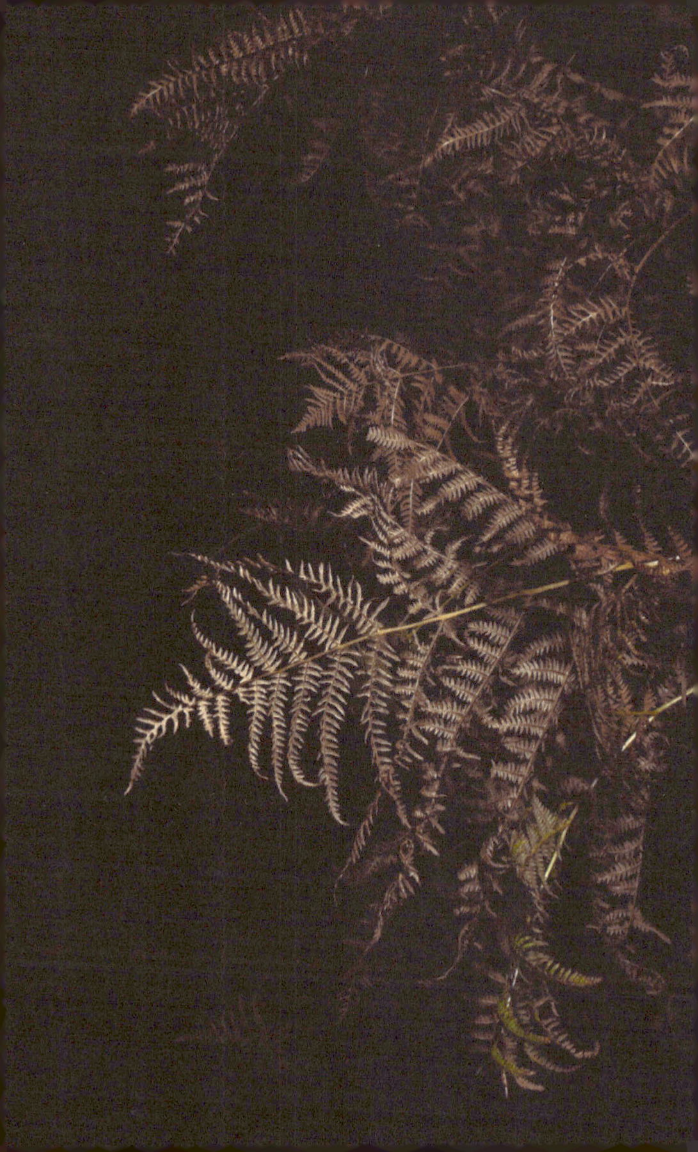

WITHIN CORNWALL'S AREA OF OUTSTANDING NATURAL Beauty, this site emerges as a hybridized biogenetic reserve, a convergence of ecological networks. It combines four prior SSSIs: Goonhilly Downs, Bray's Cot, Traboe Downs, Clahar, and Trenoon all now nested within the Lizard National Nature Reserve.

Goonhilly Downs stands approximately seven kilometres south of Helston on the Lizard Peninsula, Britain's southernmost point. The raised plateau forms the central core of the Lizard heathlands, the largest fragment of a formerly larger serpentinite heathland. The site is underlain by serpentinite, with small outcrops of granite gneiss and hornblende schist. Serpentinite is an ultra-basic rock weathering to form shallow, poorly drained gley soils. These support a basic lowland heath community dominated by Cornish heath *Erica vagans*, a Red Data Book (RDB) species in the British Isles found only on the Lizard and County Fermanagh, Northern Ireland. Scattered acrosss the serpentinite is overlain by windblown loess deposits, rises to deeper, more acidic soils supporting a calcifuge heathland vegetation. The site includes diverse heathland types, a number of pools and quarries and a system of ancient cart tracks which criss crosses the area. The atypical geology and soils found here, combined with the mild oceanic climate have caused the development of flora and fauna unique to the Lizard district.

The dominant vegetation is 'tall heath' comprising Cornish heath, black bog-rush *Schoenus nigricans* and purple moor-grass *Molinia caerulea*. Associated species include tormentil *Potentilla erecta*, saw-wort *Serratula tinctoria*, devil's-bit scabious *Succisa pratensis*, cross-leaved heath *Erica tetralix*, great burnet *Sanguisorba officinalis* and western gorse *Ulex gallii*. Common reed *Phragmites australis* often co-dominates in wetter areas where peat overlies the gleyed soils.

On the more acidic loess deposits, 'short heath' community is dominant. This comprises heather *Calluna vulgaris*, bell heather *Erica cinerea*, western gorse, purple moor-grass, cross-leaved heath and bristle bent *Agrostis curtisii*.

'Mixed heath' occurs widely throughout the site on well-drained soils. It is the most species-rich of the heathland types and is typically dominated by gorse *Ulex europaeus*, western gorse and Cornish heath with bell heather, tormentil and betony *Stachys officinalis*.

A 'wet heath' community occurs in damp pockets, often around loess deposits, comprising of Cornish heath, cross-leaved heath and purple moor-grass often in association with creeping willow Salix repens and bristle bent.

ON THE LOWER, FLATTER AREAS WITH DEEP, PEATY SOILS, a diversity of wetland habitats are apparent. Tall fen vegetation, dominated in some places by greater tussock-sedge *Carex paniculata* occurs with sharp-flowered rush *Juncus acutiflorus*, grey willow *Salix cinerea* and of particular note bogbean *Menyanthes trifoliata*, marsh lousewort *Pedicularis palustris* and royal fern *Osmunda regalis*, together with yellow iris *Iris pseudacorus*, meadowsweet *Filipendula ulmaria*, hemlock water-dropwort *Oenanthe crocata*, ragged robin *Lychnis flos-cuculi* and fool's water-cress *Apium nodiflorum*. Common reed and black bog-rush dominate stands along streams. Round- leaved sundew *Drosera rotundifolia* occurs in tussocks with common reed and *Sphagnum capillifolium*. Sea rush *Juncus maritimus* appears at its most inland site on the Lizard.

Many pools occur on the site, often the result of former quarries or bomb craters which have flooded to create open water bodies supporting a wide diversity of aquatic and semi-aquatic vegetation. Plant species include marsh pennywort *Hydrocotyle vulgaris*, common spike-rush *Eleocharis palustris*, shoreweed *Littorella uniflora*, pillwort *Pilularia globulifera* and floating club-rush *Eleogiton fluitans*. Rocky serpentinite outcrops and quarries which remain unflooded often support the RDB species land quillwort *Isoetes histrix*, dwarf rush *Juncus capitatus*, and fringed rupturewort *Herniaria ciliolata*, the nationally scarce autumn quill *Scilla autumnalis*, and wild chives *Allium schoenoprasum*.

The network of ancient cart-tracks which crosses Goonhilly Downs supports the RDB species pigmy rush *Juncus pygmaeus* and pillwort alongside the nationally scarce yellow centaury *Cicendia filiformis* and three-lobed crowfoot *Ranunculus tripartitus* as well as chaffweed *Anagallis minima* and lesser water-plantain *Baldellia ranunculoides*.

The orchid flora is especially noteworthy. Several species occur including the heath spotted-orchid *Dactylorhiza maculata* subsp. ericetorum, southern marsh-orchid *D. praetermissa*, fragrant orchid *Gymnadenia conopsea* and the green-winged orchid *Orchis morio*. Moreover, two rare heathers, the Dorset heath *Erica ciliaris* and the hybrid heath *Erica williams*, have been recorded.

The open water areas, including Croft Pascoe Pool and Bray's Cot Pool, provide an important habitat for dragonflies and diverse aquatic life. At least thirteen species have been recorded on Goonhilly Downs, including the small red damselfly *Ceriagrion tenellum* and the nationally scarce black-tailed skimmer *Orthetrum cancellatum*. The heathland attracts other invertebrates. Four RDB fly species *Fannia latipalpus*, *Tipula grisescens*, *Urophora spoliata* and *Myopa extricata* and seventeen regionally scarce species have been recorded. A rich beetle fauna includes the RDB species *Longitarsus rutilus* and *Graptodytes flavipes*. *Andrena falsifica*. A mining bee species, has also been recorded on the site.

There are several groves of mixed conifers, remnants of former plantations, now giving way to a mixed heath community. The mixture provides habitat for numerous bird species. The site is an important breeding ground for nightjar *Camprimulgus europaeus*. Other avian breeders include curlew *Numenius arquata*, lapwing *Vanellus vanellus*, stonechat *Saxicola torquata* and grasshopper warbler *Locustella naevia*. The Goonhilly site is a hunting ground for merlin *Falco columbarius*, kestrel *Falco tinnunculus*, buzzard *Buteo buteo*, short-eared owl *Asio flammeus*, barn owl *Tyto alba*, peregrine *Falco peregrinus* and hen harrier *Circus cyaneus*.

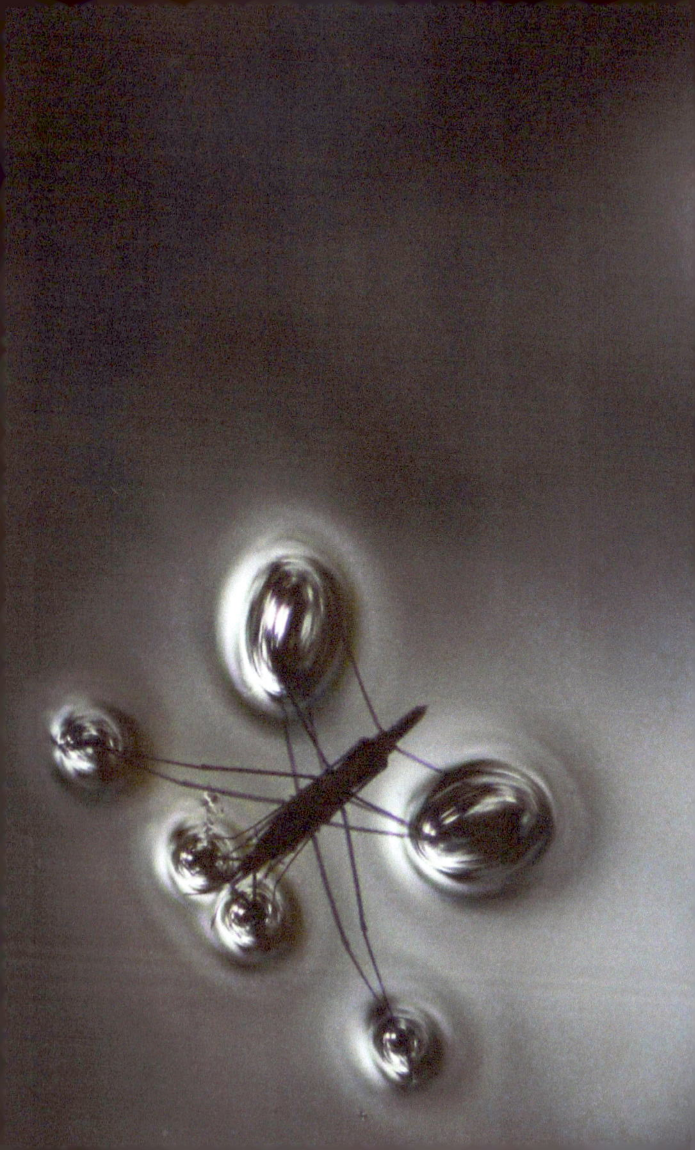

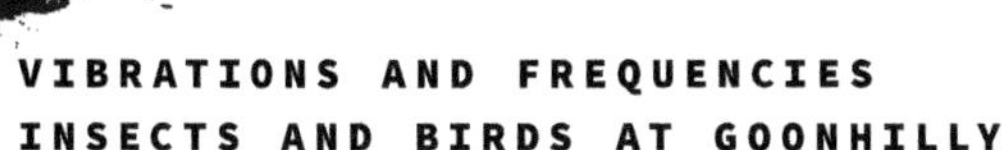

VIBRATIONS AND FREQUENCIES
INSECTS AND BIRDS AT GOONHILLY

The vibrational frequencies below are approximate and can vary depending on factors such as size, behaviour, and physiology. This is only a small example of the multitudinous lifeforms at Goonhilly.

MINER BEES: The buzzing sound produced by miner bees, unique to the downs during their flight and communication, has a frequency range of around 200-250 Hz.

BUMBLEBEES: Generate buzzing sounds with frequencies ranging from 100 to 400 Hz.

CRICKETS: Male crickets produce chirping sounds by rubbing their wings together, resulting in frequencies between 2 and 8 kHz. The chirping rate can vary among different cricket species.

GRASSHOPPERS: Grasshoppers produce a characteristic buzzing or chirping sound by rubbing their wings together. The frequency of their sounds can range from 1 to 4 kHz.

BEETLES: Some produce sounds by stridulation, which involves rubbing body parts together. The frequency can vary widely depending on the species, ranging from a few hundred Hz to several kHz.

ANTS: While most do not produce audible sounds, they can communicate through vibrations. These vibrations occur at low frequencies and are often used for alarm or recruitment purposes within colonies.

WATER BOATMAN: This tiny creature is the loudest animal on Earth relative to its body size. Its "singing" can be up to 99.2 decibels. The insect makes the sound by rubbing its genitalia against its abdomen in a process known as "stridulation". The song is a courtship display performed to attract a mate.

MOSQUITOES: A common group of aquatic insects that use vibrational frequencies for mate selection. Male mosquitoes produce a characteristic high-frequency buzzing sound by beating their wings rapidly. The frequency of mosquito wing beats can range from around 200 Hz to more than 1000 Hz.

DIVING BEETLES: Capable of producing vibrational signals to communicate and locate potential prey. Their vibrational frequencies can range from a few hundred Hz to several kHz, depending on the species.

STONEFLIES: Males of certain stonefly species produce courtship songs to attract females. These songs consist of low-frequency vibrations, typically ranging from 50 Hz to a few hundred Hz.

MAYFLIES: Known for their synchronized mating swarms, which involve the production of vibrational signals. The vibrational frequencies of mayflies can vary widely, ranging from tens to hundreds of Hz.

NIGHT JARS: About four pairs breed in the Croft Pascoe area on Goonhilly. Their songs have an an average pulse in the churring occupies a space between 1.04 KHz and 2.8 KHz, the abnormal pulses here are truncated at around 1.5 KHz. Some have ghostly upper portions, extending fractionally higher than expected, to 2.96 KHz.

SOIL REVERBERATIONS

Soil functions as a living, dynamic system where organisms contribute to its structure, fertility, and the broader ecosystem by generating vibrational frequencies. These sounds, resonating through the Earth's crust, influence energy flow between the biosphere and geosphere. A "noisy" soil indicates health, and these sounds can be recorded and measured to assess soil conditions, offering a unique way to evaluate ecological health.

EARTHWORMS: Commonly found in the topsoil or the organic-rich surface layer, produce vibrational signals as they move through the soil. These can range from a few Hz to several kHz, depending on the size and activity of the earthworms.

SOIL ARTHROPODS: Various soil-dwelling arthropods, such as mites, springtails, and centipedes, generate vibrations as they crawl, feed, or interact with their environment. The vibrational frequencies produced by these organisms can range from a few hundred Hz to several kHz.

SOIL BACTERIA: Bacteria are present throughout the soil horizons and play crucial roles in nutrient cycling and decomposition processes. While they do not produce audible sounds, they generate microscopic vibrations as they move or interact with their surroundings. These vibrations occur at extremely low frequencies, typically below the range of human hearing.

SOIL NEMATODES: Microscopic roundworms found in various soil horizons, move through the soil matrix and interact with other organisms. They generate vibrations as they swim, feed, or search for food sources. The vibrational frequencies produced by nematodes can range from a few hundred Hz to a few kHz.

NOTE

I have recorded these vibrations using contact microphones (to amplify the vibrational worlds of microorganisms) and geophones, to extend my hearing and perception to more-than-human worlds, typically beyond the range of human perception.

As an art practice mud is a way to attune to the materiality of a site engaging fine and gross motor skills, sensory awareness, balance and coordination. These practices open up the sensorium to other bodies and ways of working.

FREQUENCY BANDS COMMONLY USED BY SATELLITES AT GOONHILLY EARTH STATION

VERY HIGH FREQUENCY (VHF): Range from 30 to 300 MHz and are often used for satellite communications, including amateur radio and some satellite downlinks.

ULTRA-HIGH FREQUENCY (UHF): Range from 300 MHz to 3 GHz and are commonly used for various applications, including television broadcasting, mobile satellite services, and satellite phones.

C-BAND: Range from 3.7 to 4.2 GHz for downlink and 5.9 to 6.4 GHz for uplink. This frequency band is widely used for satellite communication, including television distribution, telecommunications, and data services.

KU-BAND: Range from 11 to 18 GHz for downlink and 14 to 14.5 GHz for uplink. This frequency band is commonly used for satellite television broadcasting, broadband internet access, and other communication services.

KA-BAND: Range from 26.5 to 40 GHz for downlink and 29 to 31 GHz for uplink. This frequency band is increasingly used for broadband satellite communication, including high-speed internet access and data transmission.

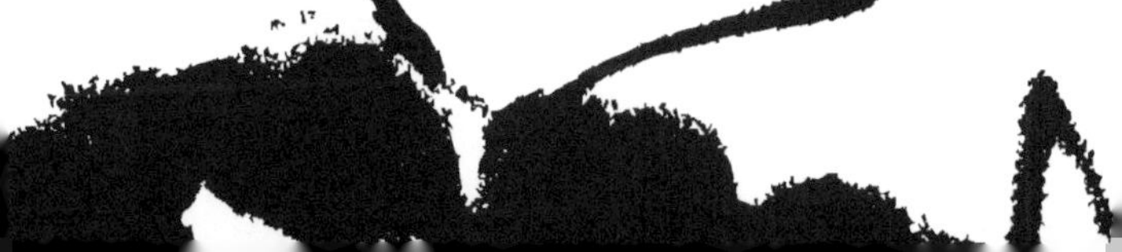

**

Ever since my childhood, radio communications have always piqued my interest, listening to a slew of hisses, white noise, radio squelch and cross channels of AM/SW radio. During my time at Goonhilly Earth Station I bought a Software-defined Radio (SDR), and VLF scanner and started undertaking sonic experiments in attempt to further understand more-than-human communication which includes the satellites, insect, and vegetal life that are transmitting and receiving.

An SDR is a radio communication system where components that have been traditionally implemented in hardware are, instead, implemented by means of software. Components such as modulators, demodulators, and tuners that are traditionally implemented in analogue hardware components, can, nowadays, be implemented in software by leveraging technology such as analogue-to-digital converters (ADC). SDR technology has several use-cases since it enables changing radio protocols in real-time while using the same hardware.

I have explored the potential of environmental agencies at Goonhilly and sensing abilities to attune to various transmissions of natural phenomenon to cultivate novel perspectives on comprehending and responding to climate change. The transmission of natural phenomenon is a distinction that Renato Romero describes as "Radio-Nature which encompasses all electromagnetic signal emissions which originated from natural phenomena, such as storms, aurora, solar wind and other events" (Romero, 2009:13). By using VLF receivers alongside bio and eco acoustics I was able to listen to ecosystems across terrestrial geomagnetic fields of the Earth, making audible a seemingly silent environment. These radio signals or atmospheric patterns, provide insights into environmental changes and offer opportunities for monitoring and analysis.

WAVES AND ANTENNAS

Radio waves are used in the satellite antenna supports at Goonhilly Earth station, applications including radio astronomy, commercial satellite communications, space situational awareness and deep space communications, making it a critical part of the world's first private deep space communications network for space communications and quantum computing. Radio waves are a subset of electromagnetic radiation with wavelengths in the electromagnetic spectrum longer than infrared light, which can be artificially generated by transmitters using antennas.

Different frequencies of radio waves have different propagation characteristics in the Earth's atmosphere; long waves can diffract around obstacles like mountains and follow the contour of the earth (ground waves), shorter waves can reflect off the ionosphere and return to earth beyond the horizon (skywaves), while much shorter wavelengths bend or diffract very little and travel on a line of sight, so their propagation distances are limited to the visual horizon.

In a sense the amateur radio community has been using space ever since they learned to bounce signals off the ionosphere to reach other hams far beyond the horizon. It seems natural that they eventually continued on above this thin barrier. Satellites communicate by exchanging electromagnetic waves, either on the Earth's surface or in space, hovering above a pole or orbiting us every day.

Satellites use different parts of the electromagnetic (EM) spectrum depending on their mission. Communications satellites primarily use the radio spectrum, and within that satellite operators choose the frequency that best suits their needs. In many cases, different spectrums can be used on a single satellite. For instance, a communications satellite may manage data uplink and downlink in one band but use another frequency for TT&C (telemetry, tracking and command)..

SPECULATIVE FIELD STUDY
(DEEP SPACE ECOSYSTEMS)

Celestial messengers in Cornish bogs.

Orbiting beacons emerge in reflected wetlands.

Cosmic voyagers and rare heaths.

The luminous sentinel's prehistoric lizards.

Astral ancestors layered with peat crofting,
and submerged ecosystems.

Radiant collaborators.

Spaceborne embers.

Echoes of the universe oscillate through
the soil horizon.

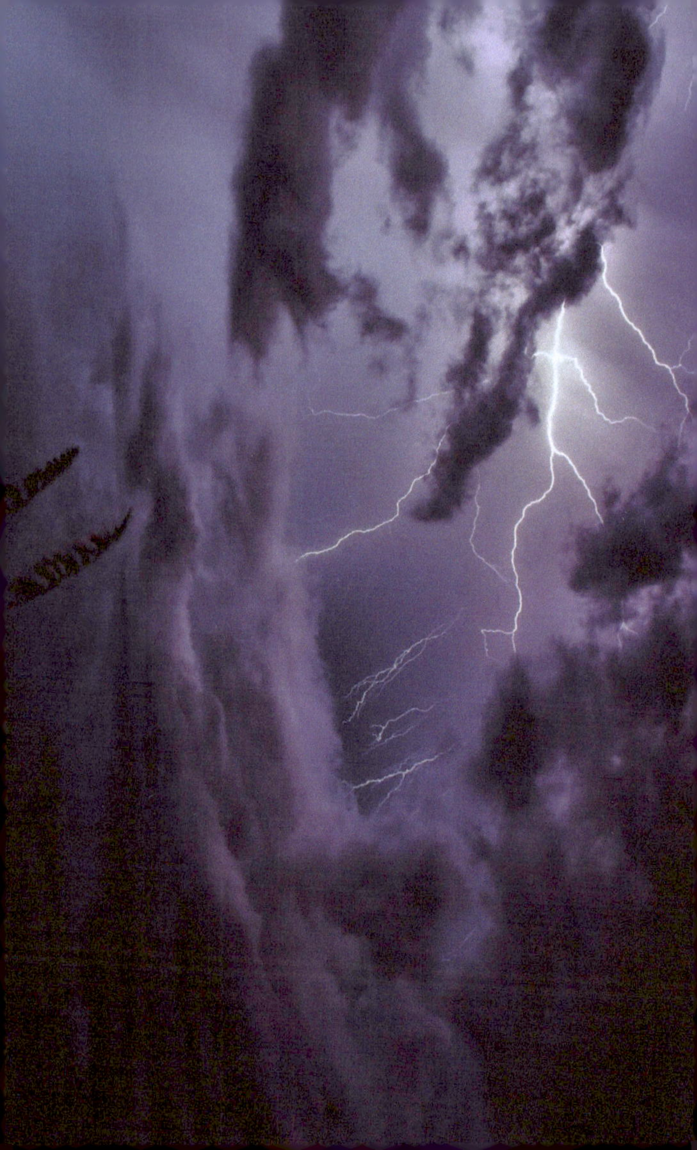

SPECULATIVE FIELD STUDY
(EARTH SONICS)

Lightning aftershocks in the sky overhead.

Photons radiating an atmospheric spectacle.

Spherics illuminate the heavens
with ethereal light.

Broadband impulses in the electric air,
natural earth oscillations.

Lightning storms from across the world
resonating along grey line propagation.

Unfolding a sonic landscape deep
in the strata, fissures, and plates of the earth.

Earth-ionosphere waveguide.

A cosmic message in a surge of rapture.

In the time-domain, a single spike.

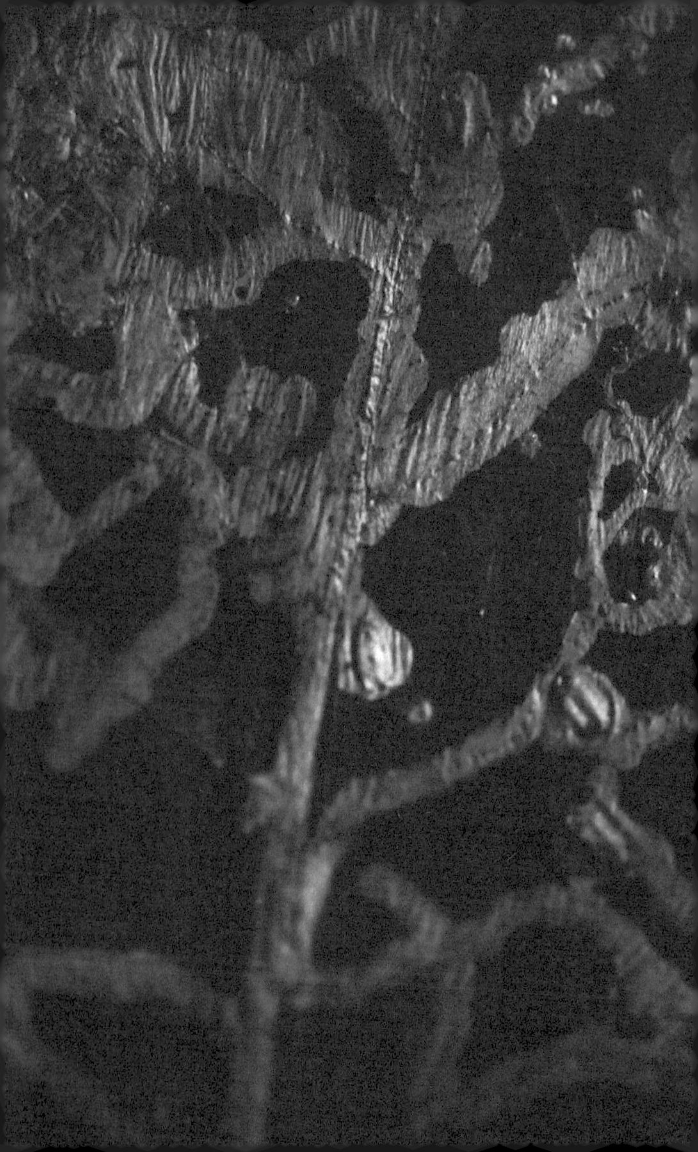

SPECULATIVE FIELD STUDY
(STINK BUG)

Pheromones / scents secreted through animal
architectures.

Acrid, earthy musk.

Thorax filled with odorous glands.

Danger calls, chemical release.

Exoskeleton discharges through the evapatorium.

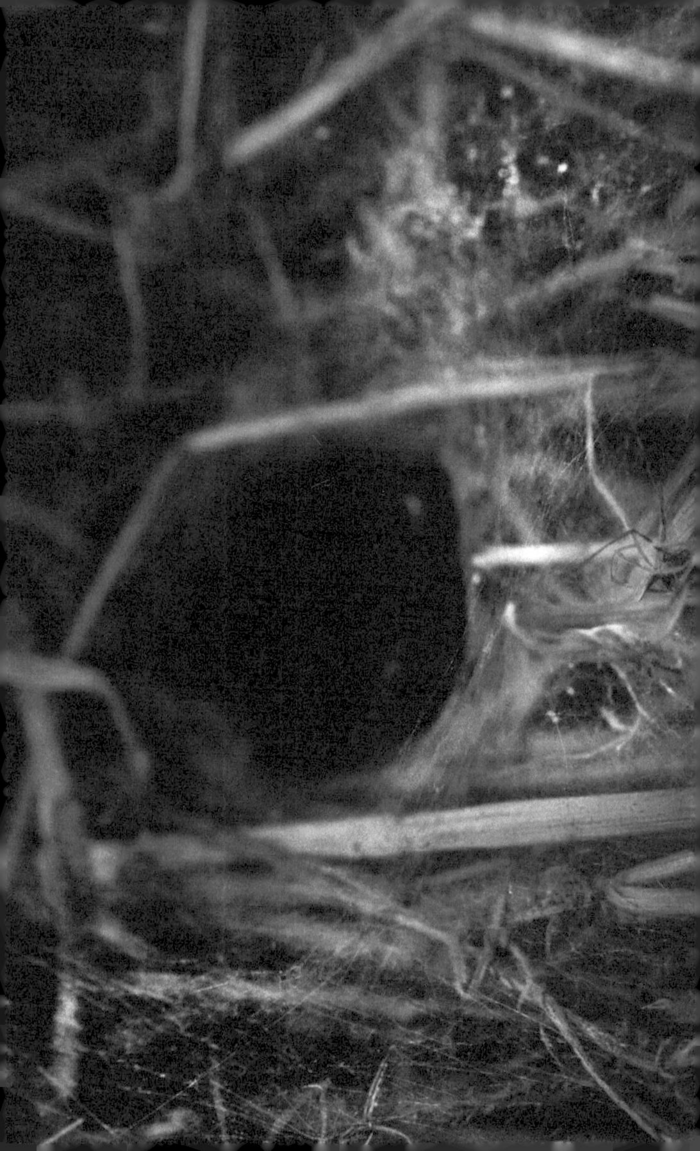

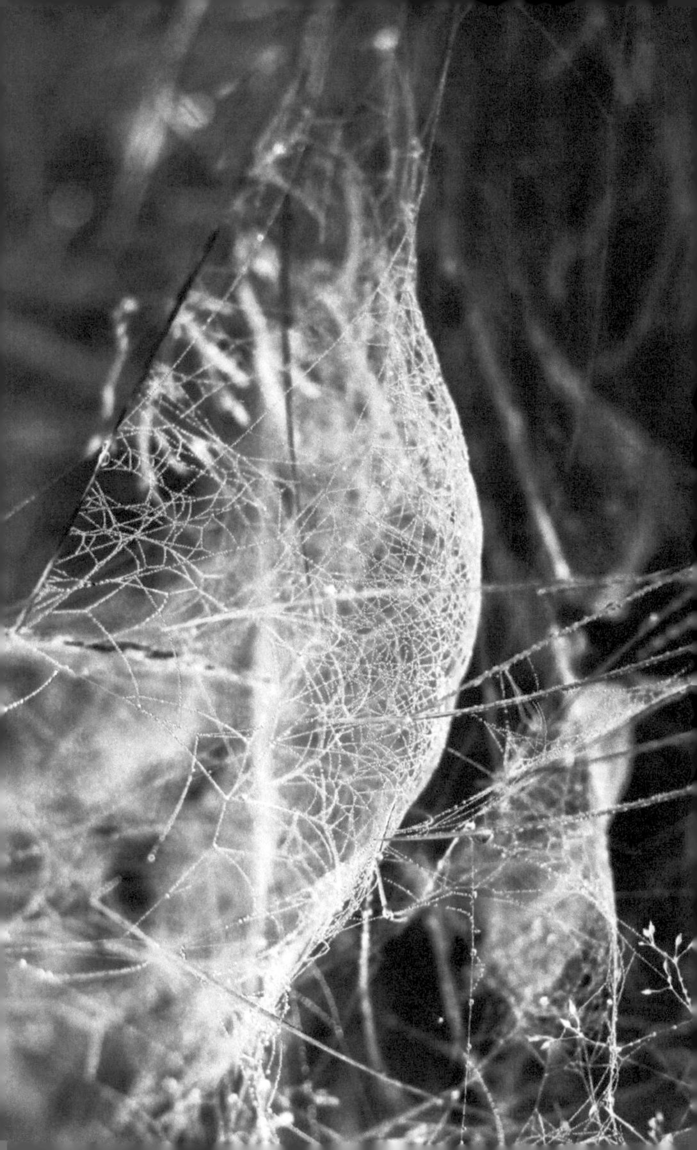

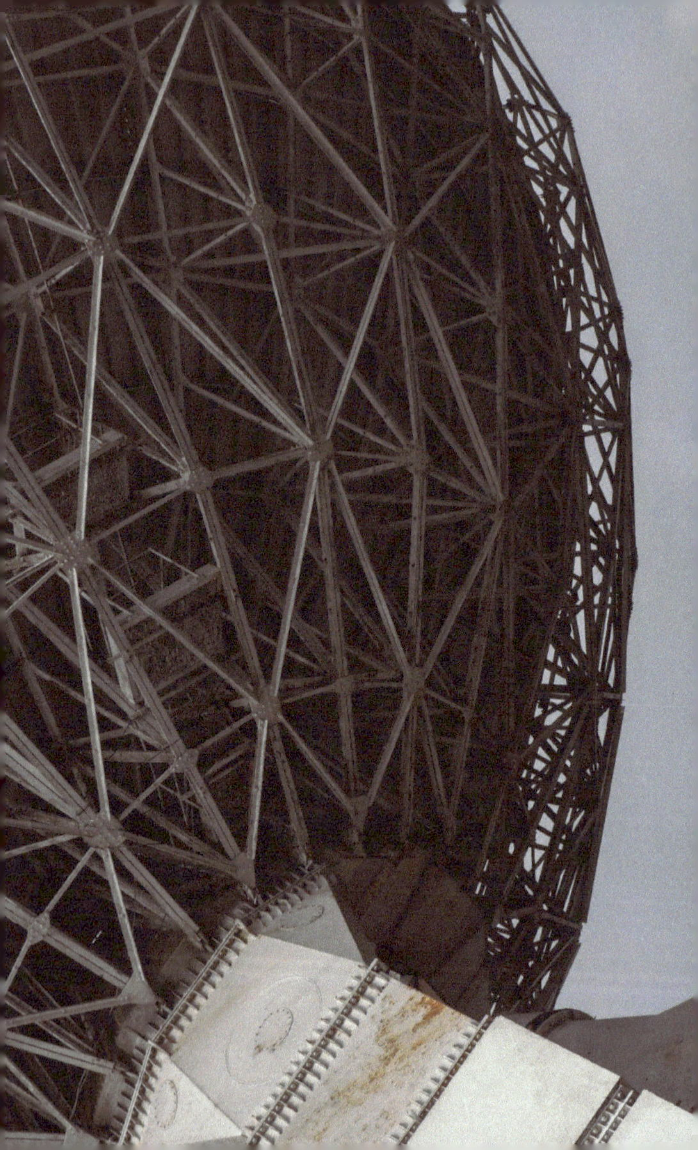

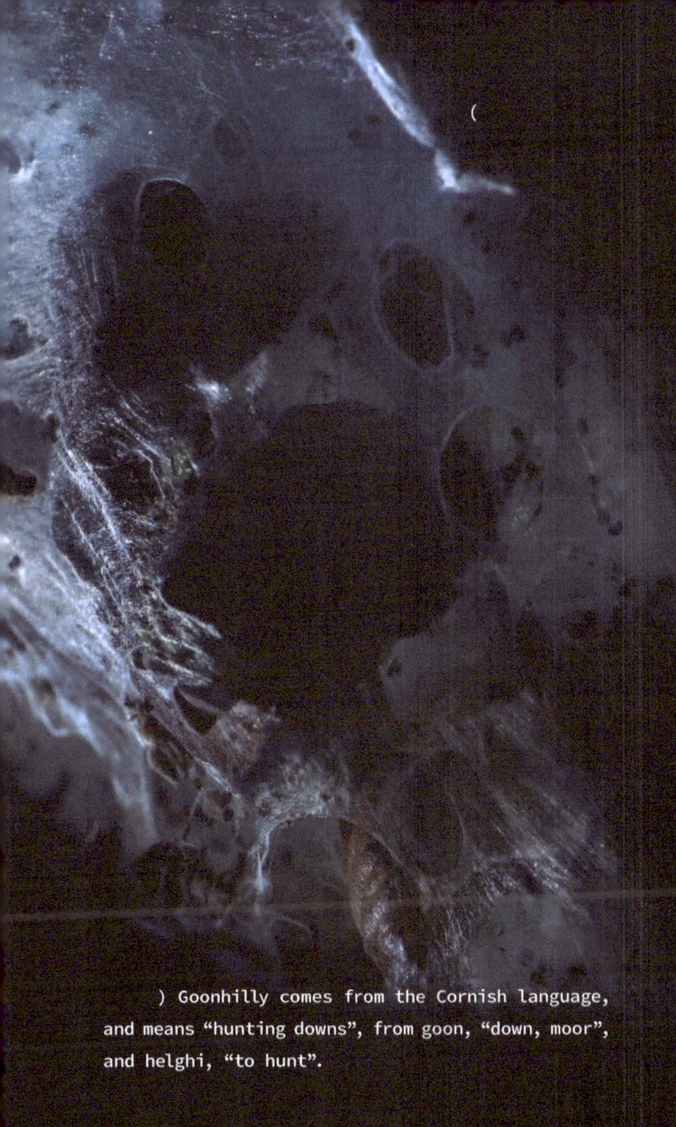

(

) Goonhilly comes from the Cornish language, and means "hunting downs", from goon, "down, moor", and helghi, "to hunt".

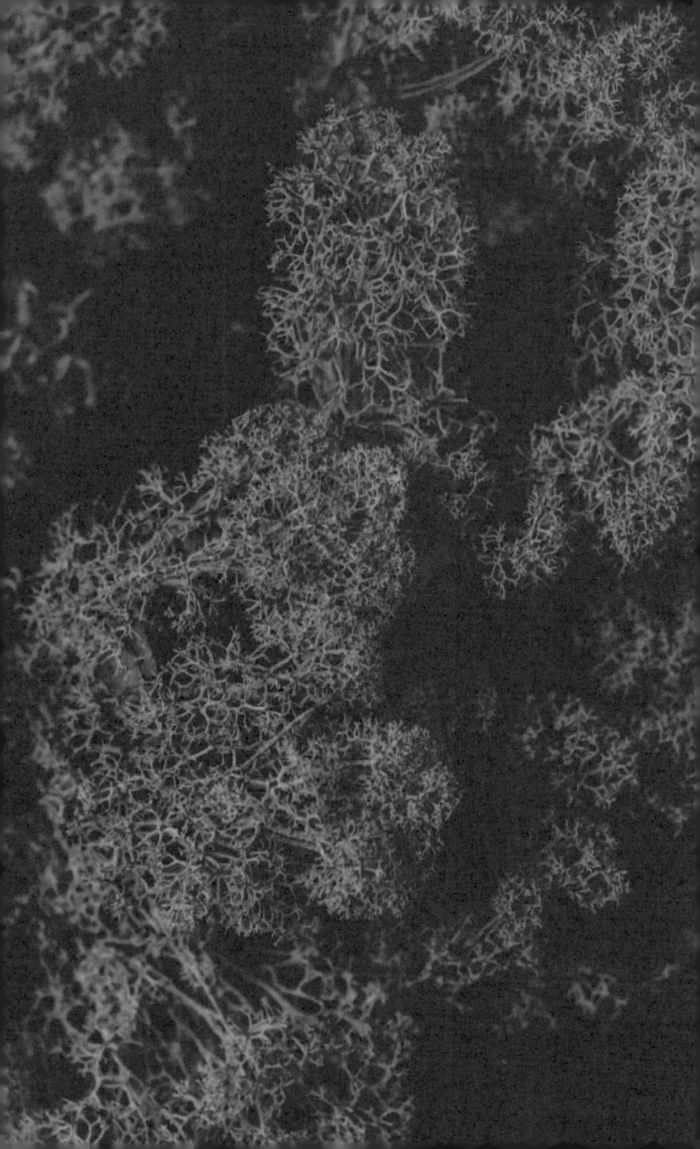

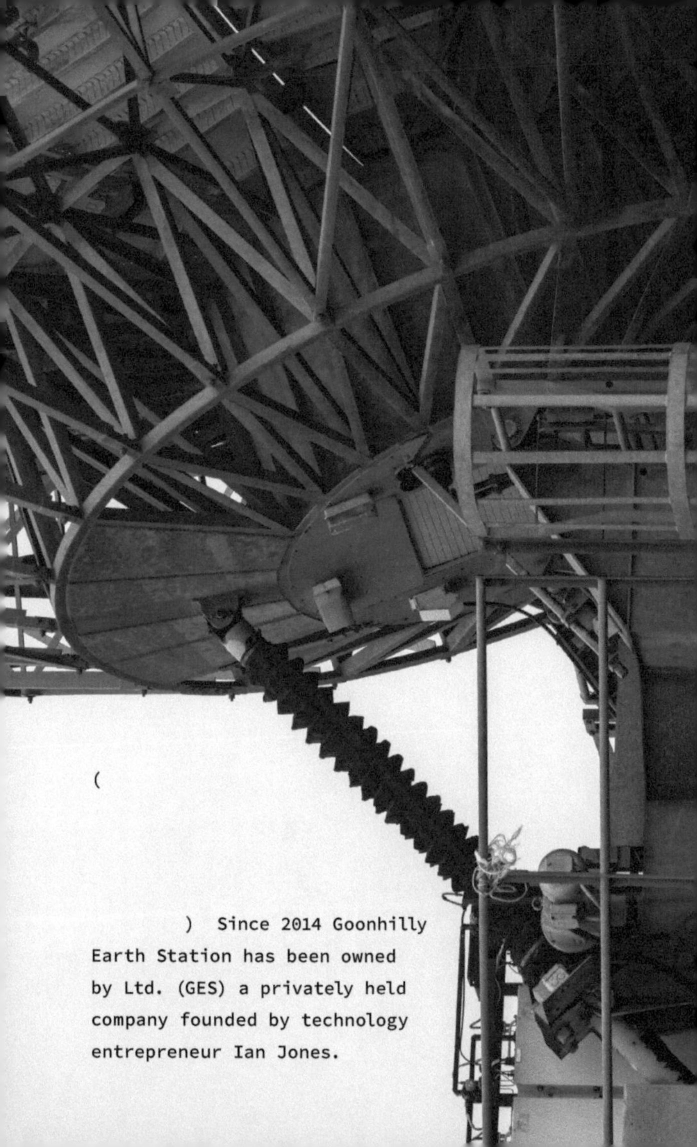
(
) Since 2014 Goonhilly
Earth Station has been owned
by Ltd. (GES) a privately held
company founded by technology
entrepreneur Ian Jones.

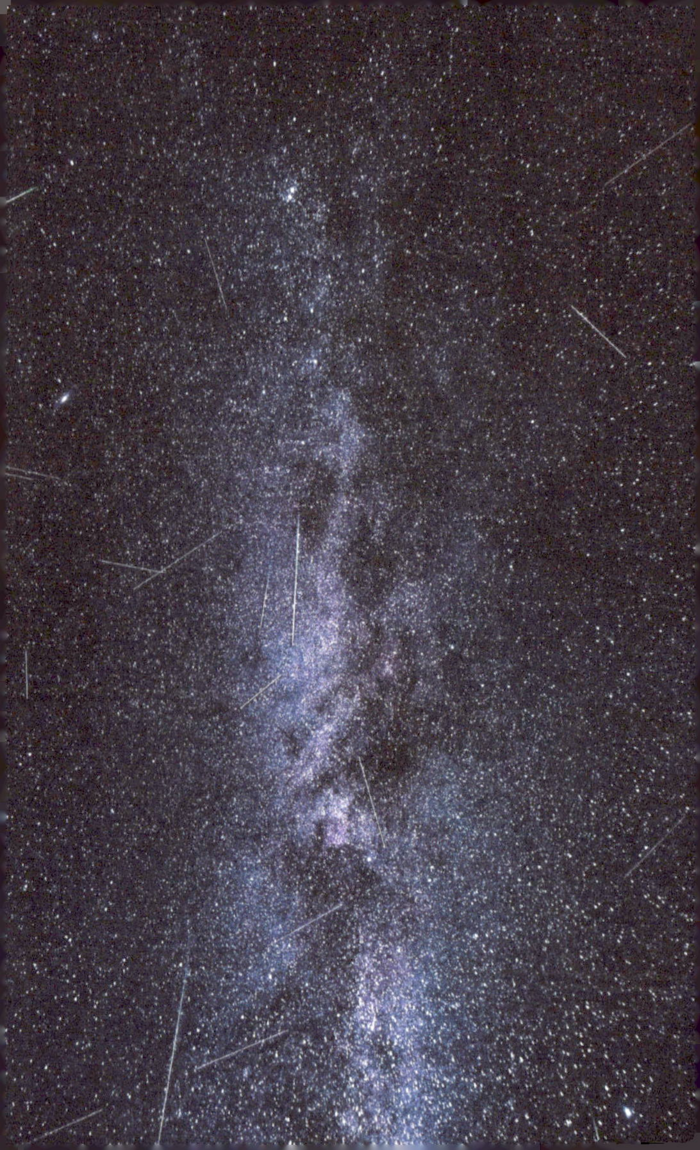

A blue twilight haze cast over the mostly flooded
downs. (

) At night, in the midst of the dreary waste,
the form of a ghostly vessel may be seen floating with lug-sails spread out on Croft Pasco Pool,
amongst the leeches and water boatmen walking above
the high surface tension of the water. (

)

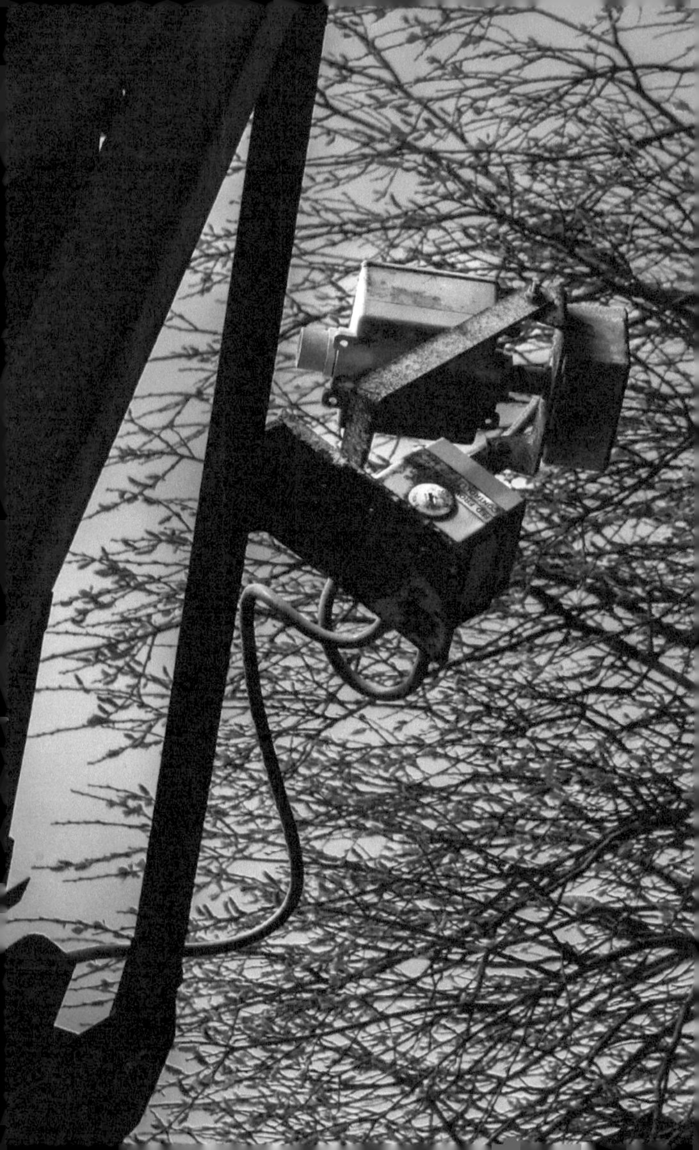

GROUND WAVES

Speculative field recording test piece.
Goonhilly Downs SSSI Installation in situ

Pouring out VLF, UHF radios, buried on site, looped, strapped to pillars and posts, hidden beneath trees, safe from sun and rain, strapped to a scaffold pole hung from the sky, installed in the WW2 bunker where signals were decoded. Sonic essay on insect and satellite communication dragged from a Neolithic bog and transmitted into deep space, allowed to come back to earth through the misty unknowns of the downs, the common-place forgotten tones of a century falling in on itself, fragments of music, beamed back amongst the quagmire, an imaginary voiceover. Soundscapes of thresholds and conduits, time and space, exit plans and lost rocks, living, insects communication, copulating and surviving, trying to tie us all together, before we fall apart.

Ground waves are taken as a constant in a world of change, whose magnetic end points flip and flop along a timeline that extends beyond our present frame of reference. That's north over there, that's south, all perspective, from Neolithic standing stones, rebalanced by Victorian visitors, to Napoleonic crofters who became English through a sheer determination and an unwillingness to leave;

from appropriated scientific technology for nostalgic whimsies and misinterpretation, everything we have ever beamed from the surface of the earth is still going, into the vacuum of black holes on the furthest edges of a universe we can now confirm looks exactly like you expected, and nothing like you imagined.

GROUND WAVES is a transmissional sound installation test piece where teleportations are made, and thresholds breached, amongst the brush and the bog, and the sweeping rain, where you'll hear fragments of pilot projects, of thrills and outlandish suggestions, strange endeavours scantly recorded, and hidden amongst the quagmire.

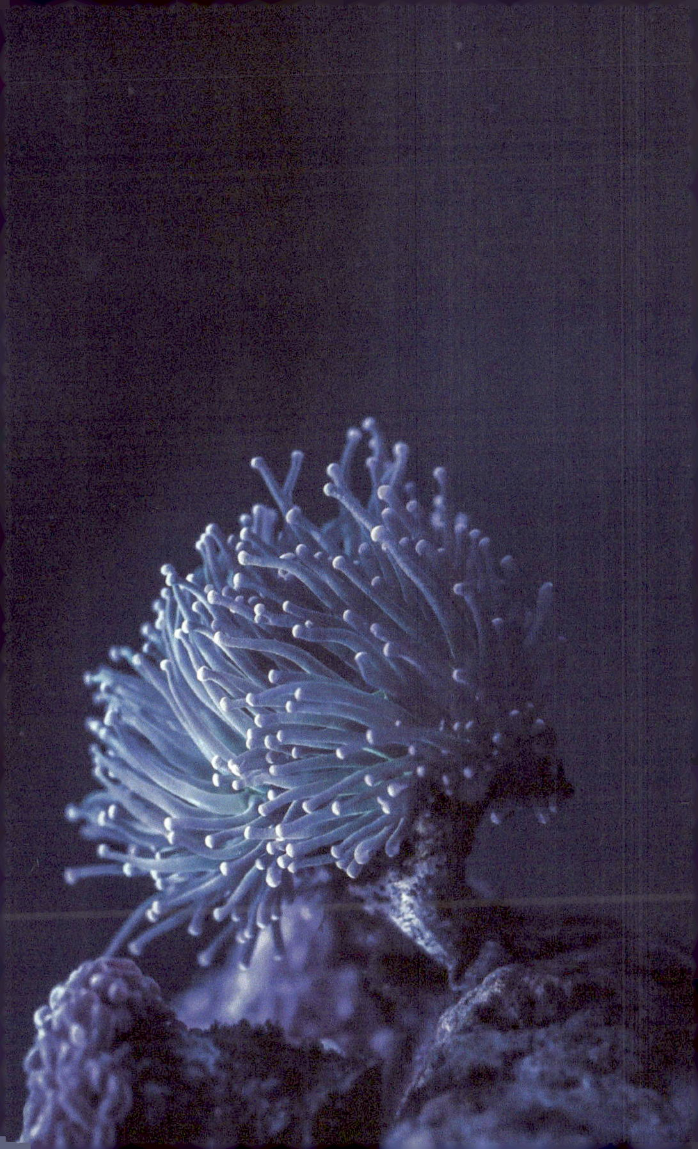

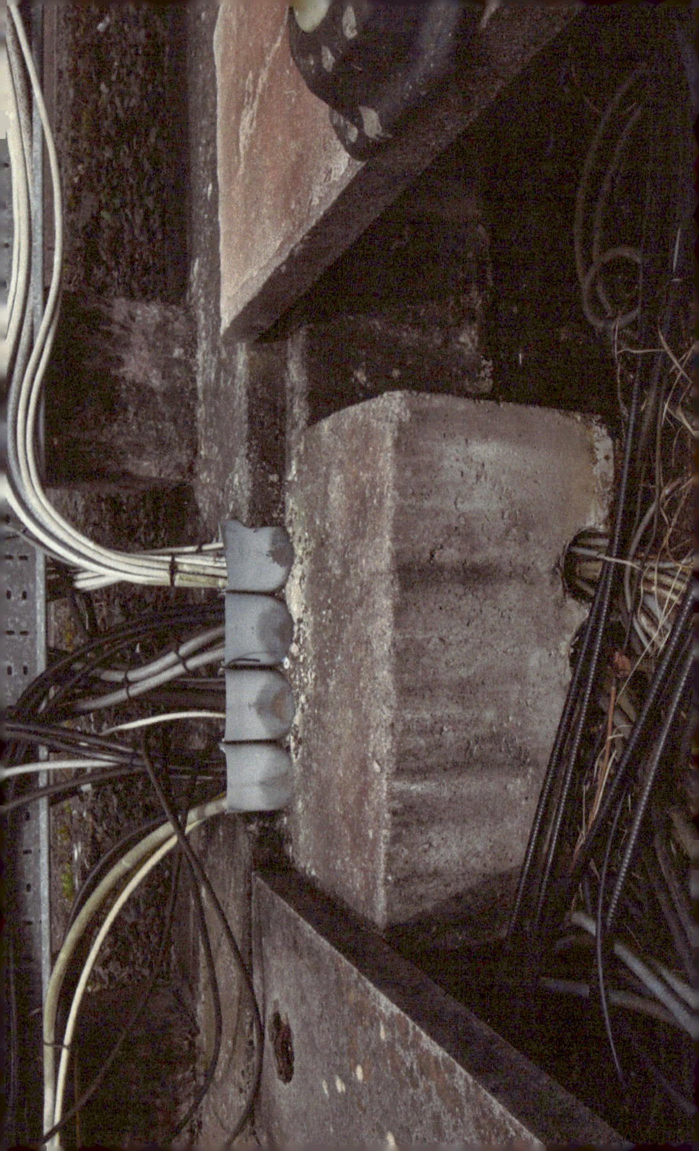

SPECULATIVE FIELD STUDY
(CROFTING THE DOWNS)

Small holdings 'crofts' made by local farmers.

Enclosed areas of land within larger commons, remnants of where they cut turf, collected furze and grazed cattle. What's left of two 19th century crofts, Croft Noweth and the Dry Tree Croft are still visible through the Cornish drizzle.

In the rugged terrain, ancient myths, land scarred by history, lies Goonhilly Downs, where memories have long been buried.

Crofters would venture out, their hands calloused. Tilling the soil, unforgiving acidic serpentine soils littered with granite.

Their labours nurtured the land. A patchwork of fields, where generations stewarded the earth.

SPECULATIVE FIELD STUDY
(BARROWS)

Scrubby hedges leafless trees.

Barren expanses.

Hidden, entangled in the bramble and heath.

Unfarmed since the Bronze Age.

The three barrows of Mawgan-in-Meneage,
close to the north-east perimeter fence.

In the background is the kerbed barrow just to the
NNE of the Dry Tree Menhir, a ditch that surrounds
the slight mound the stone stands on.

Megalithic architectures hidden in the overgrowth.

Cruc Draenoc burial chamber one barrow near
Dry Tree menhir.

Access difficult, two large stones stand on either
side of the mound, one slightly obscured.

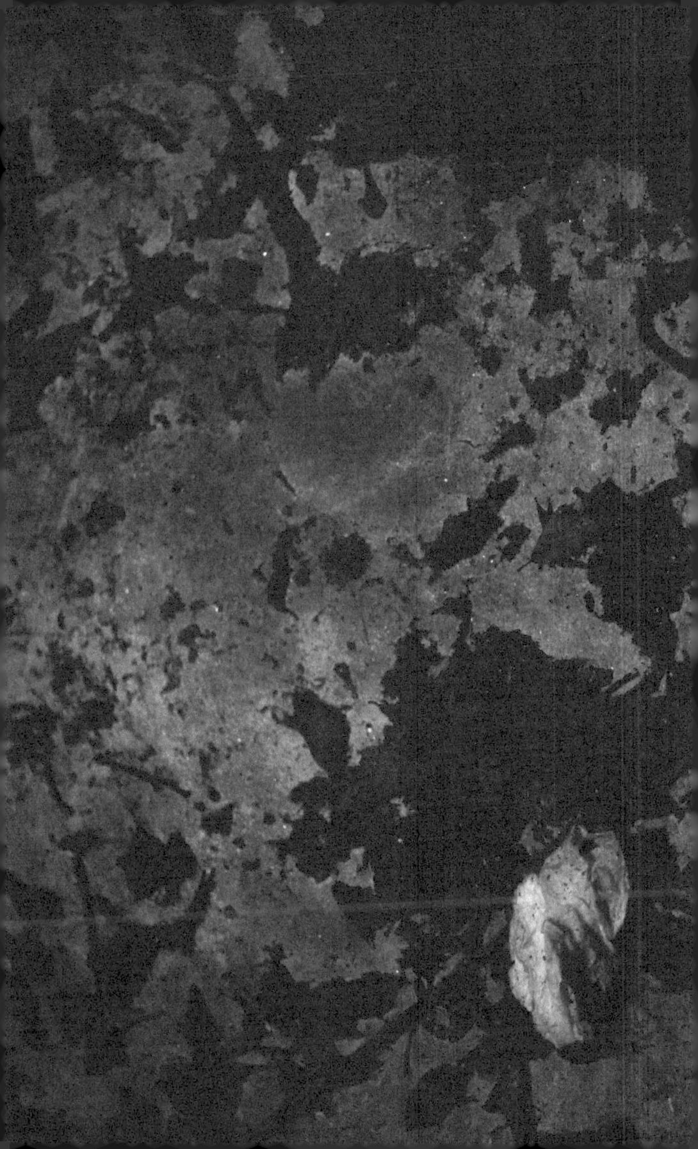

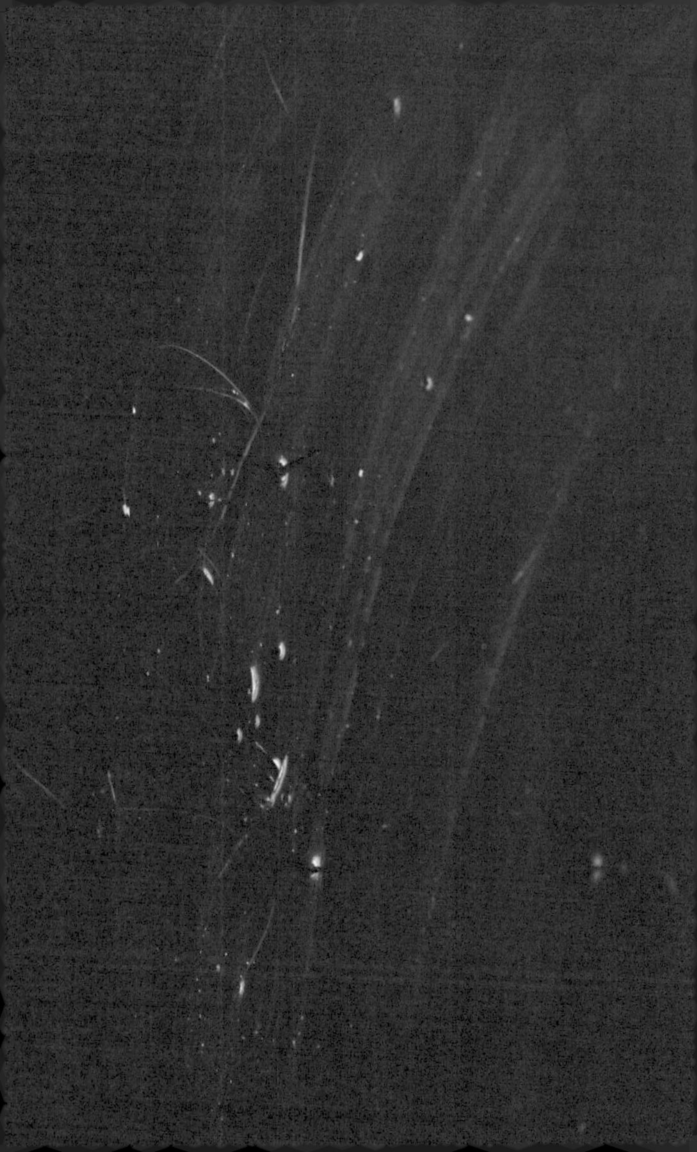

NOCTURNAL FIELD STUDY

AZMUTH ANGLE: 30 E
SATELLITE: GHY-1

Approaching the viewing platform through a narrow labyrinth of alleyways, I noticed the gates were open to the signals room—the Happidrome.

As I forebodingly breached the threshold into the dark space, I entered a structure which had signs of graffiti and violence, bricks smashed and holes forcefully made in the walls, which were part of RAF Dry Tree.

The receiver block was the nerve center, which provides access to the roof overlooking the GHY-1 satellite and the mounds of Goonhilly Downs. These mounds were designed as a landscape intervention during WW2 to prevent airplanes from landing.

Small letterbox windows overgrown with brambles and hawthorn formed a serpent's tail. The exposed window gave sight to a near-perfect swarth of the nearby ex-British telecom recreation ground.

RAF Dry Tree was a Chain Home Radar Station constructed in 1940 to detect aircraft approaching South Cornwall and the Western Approaches. The site had four 110m transmitter masts and two 73m wooden receiver towers.

Many attacks were nocturnally detected by Dry Tree and Trelanvean who in turn sent intercepting Beaufighters and Mosquito's from nearby RAF Predannack.

Predannack is located near and is visible from the site on the horizon. Dripping water resonates throughout the large eerie space haunted by war.

The nearby area housed another three radar bases and an airfield at RAF Predannack, where a myriad of creatures have been reported. Adders in the undergrowth, rare and sporadically scurrying lizards.

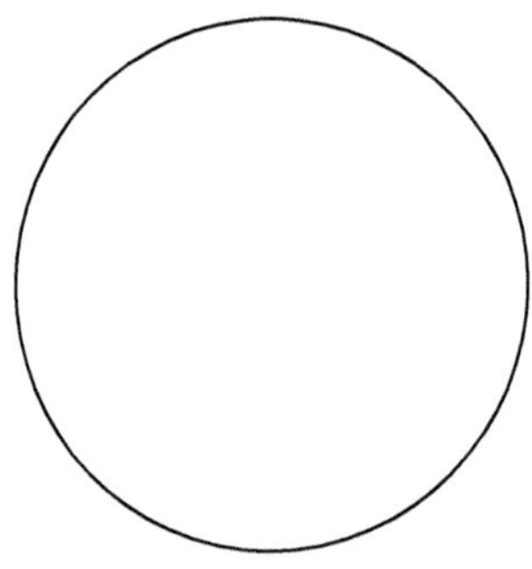

I have only witnessed leeches darting in puddles, stirring the mud into cosmic deep space renderings of a sediment nebulae.

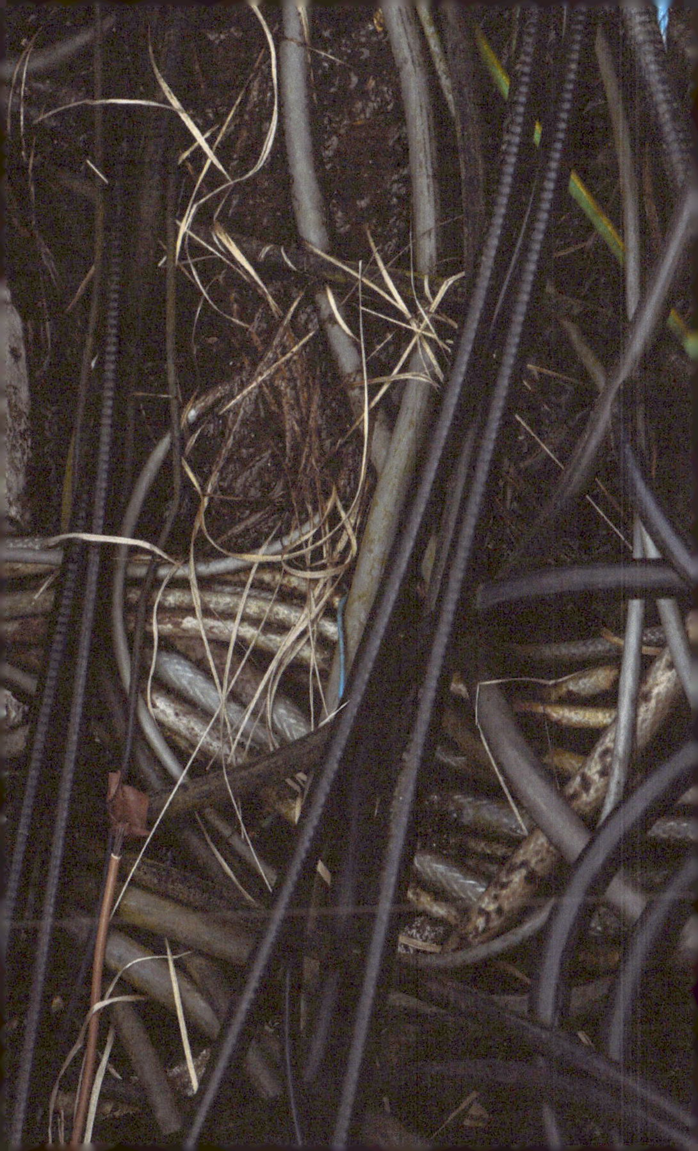

NOCTURNAL FIELD STUDY

AZMUTH ANGLE: 10 W
SATELLITE: GHY-1

Breaching the thresholds of flat dimensions,
searching for the other.

Verticality, space extending through the material
plane.

Structures indeterminate.

Concrete megaliths, granite schists and fissures.
Shifting surfaces and depths.

Enveloped in inert minerals, soil and waste,
layers of data and serpentine geology.

Cable systems and operators.

Entangled fibre optic networks.

Submarine Cable Landing Stations.

A matrix of subsea cables—SeaMeWe-3, UK-Channel
Islands 8—connecting the world to this fractal
Cornish plateau.

NOCTURNAL FIELD STUDY

AZMUTH ANGLE: 10 W Satellite: GHY-1

In a strange moment of realisation, something becomes
perceptible beyond the landscape's materiality.

Horizon and earth merge.

The airwaves thick and heavy with frequencies
almost tangible.

Signals unknown, experimental deep space radio
frequencies vibrating in the air, making grasses
and reeds quiver with resonant cymatics.

Foggy recollections of listening to shortwave static
on my radio as a child, spending hours with my now
deceased father waiting for alien blips and peaks.

White void of air beneath my feet.

Inorganic ascension.

Explorers of the unknown, the intangible,
the ineffable, the shadows.

Incursions in the strata.

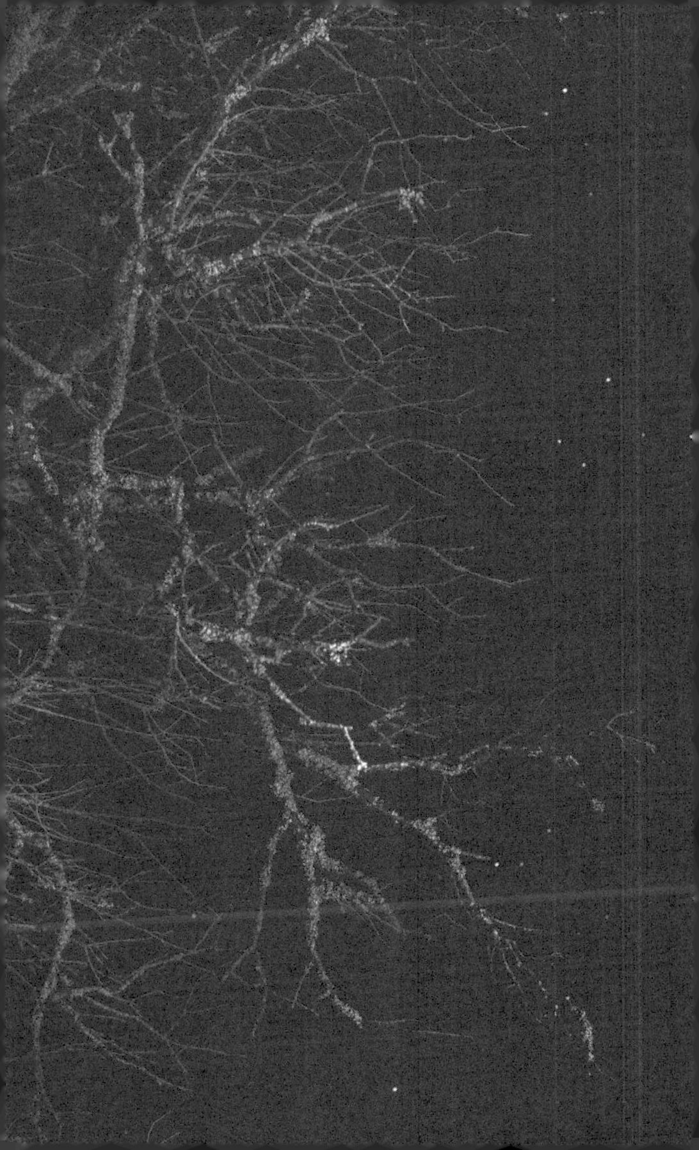

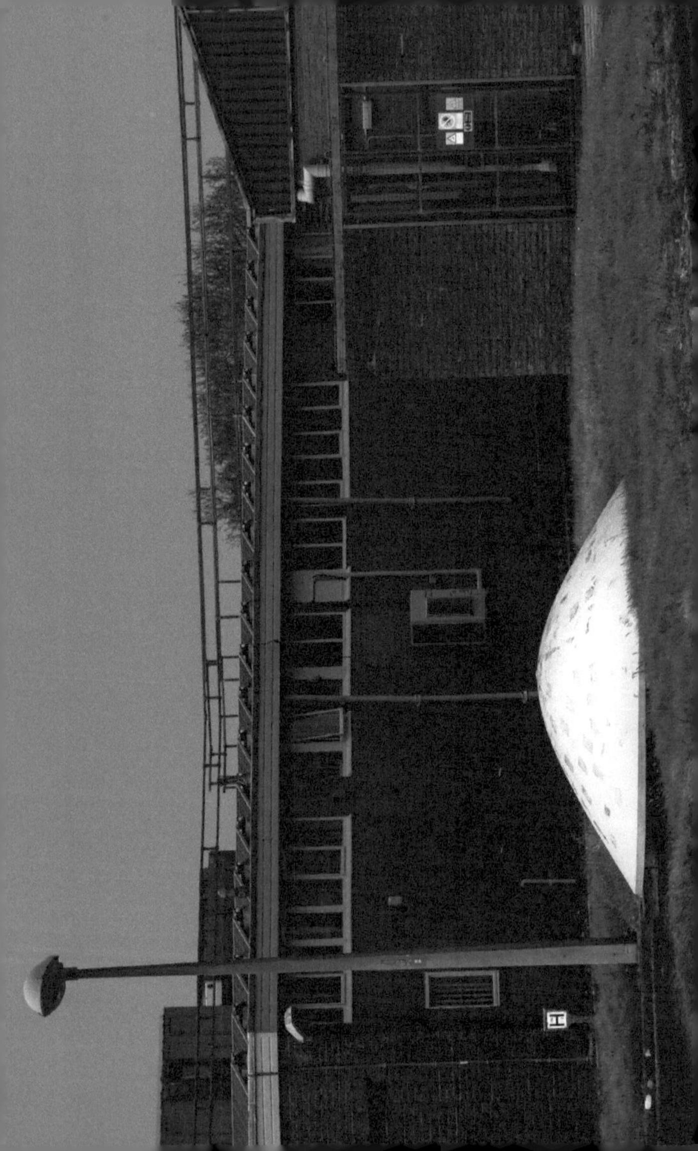

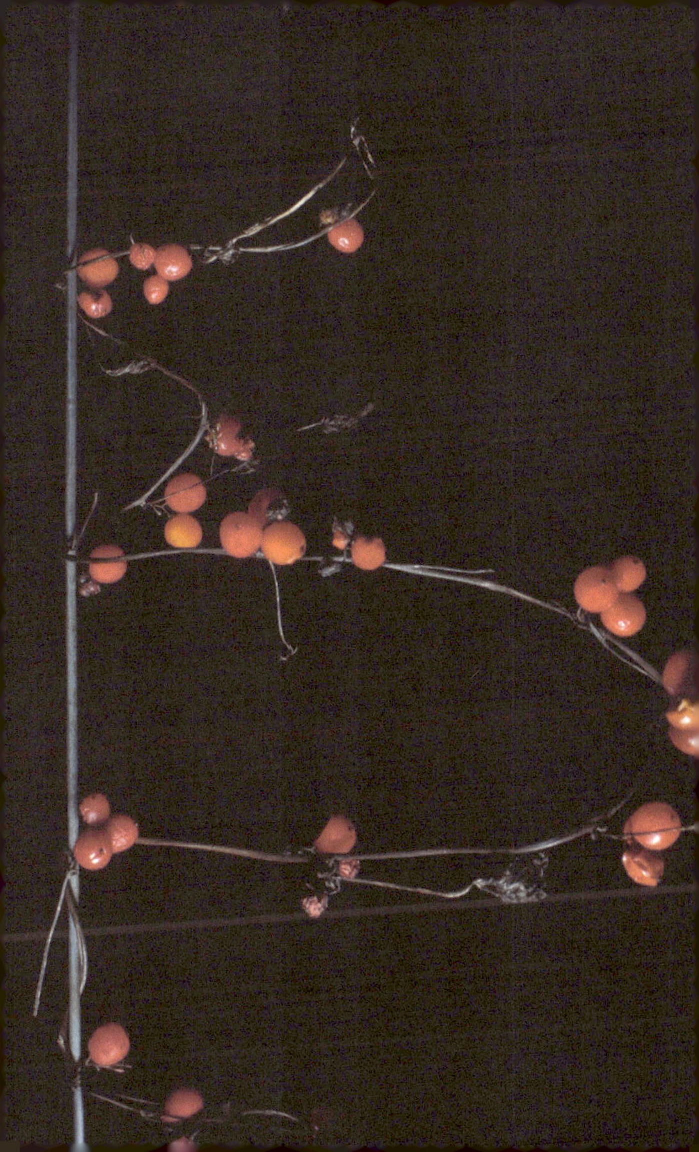

NOCTURNAL FIELD STUDY

Wet, peat-soaked bogs of watery bodies.

Squelching through aquatic life.

Breath is steam in the air; my fingers
are numb from the cold rain.

Serpentine geologic fabrics woven between
ponds and barrows.

A strange otherworldly submerged heathland.

Bracken and gorse violently and forcefully
crashing in the strong winds.

I witnessed lightning, brilliant flashes of
visible light in the form of black-body radiation.

The trees, the horizon briefly illuminated by
active photons.

I stood on the ancient burial mound overlooking
the wind turbine farm.

I waited for the thunder's shockwave, but just
an overwhelming silence enveloped the landscape.

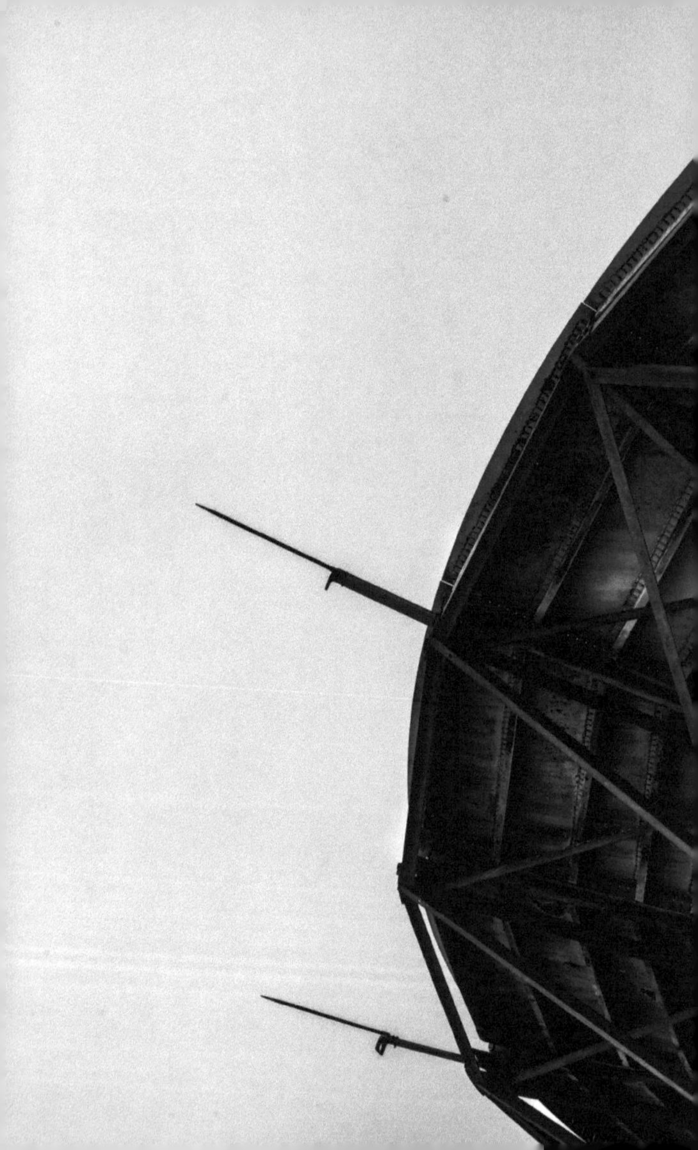

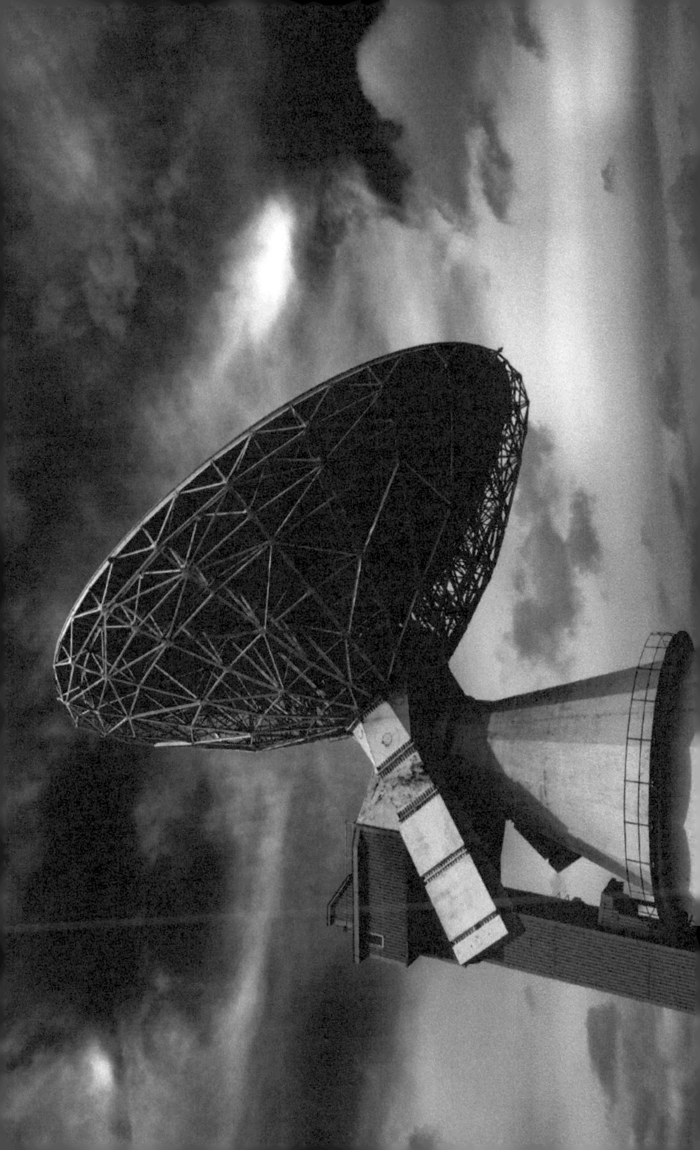

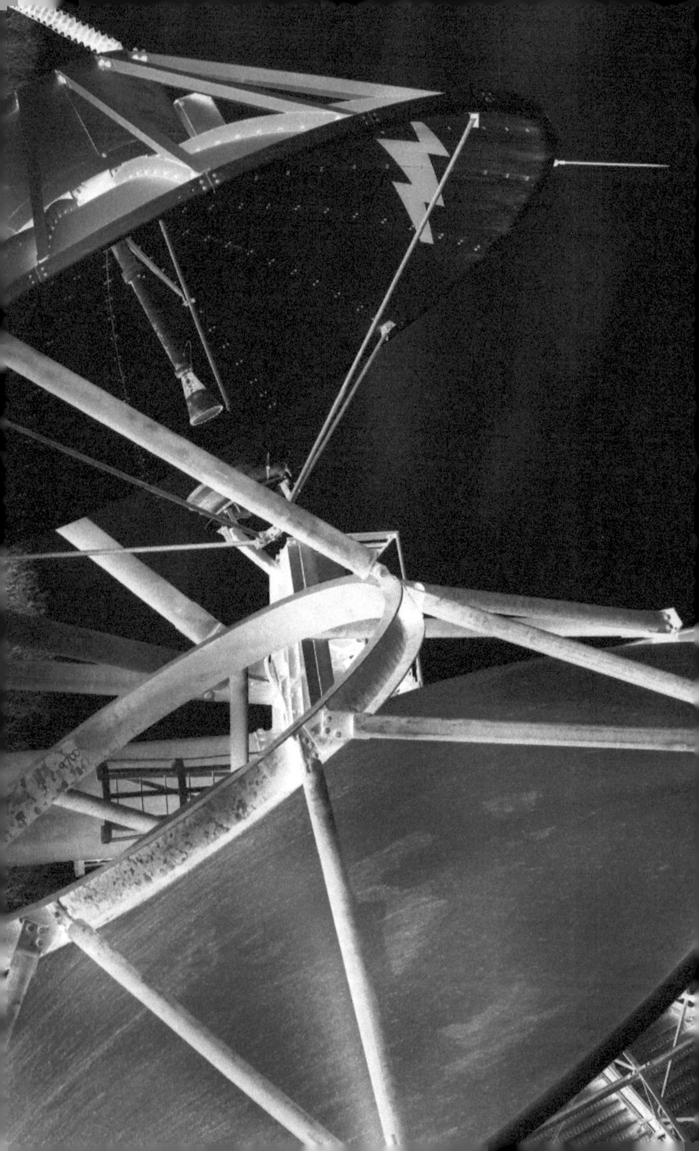

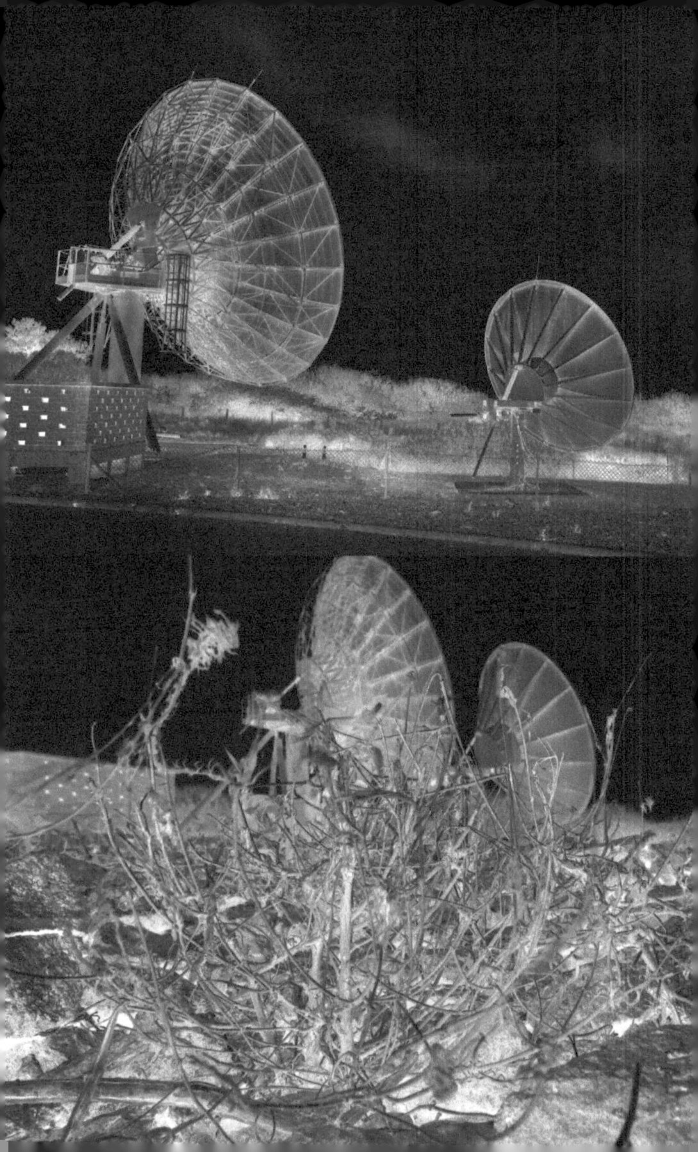

NOCTURNAL FIELD STUDY

AZMUTH ANGLE: 10 W

SATELLITE: GHY-1

Text converted to morse code

·— ···· —· —· ··· · ·——· ··—— ··· —·—· ·· · ··· — ······
—— ·· ·— —· ···· · —· ·——· —· ··· ··· · · —— ——— ·—
·—· ·· ···· ·—— ·— · ·——· ·—· ··· — · · ·—· · —— ·—— ·
·—· ·· · —·—· —— ··· —·—· —— · ·——· ·— · —— —— —·
·—· ·· —·—· —— ·—— · ··· · ·——· · —— ·—·—·· ·—— · ·
·· ·· · — ·—· —— ·—— · —· ·· · · —· ·· · ·—·
·—· · ·· ·——· · —·—· ·—· ·—— —— —· · ·—— —— ——
·—— ·—— ··· —· ·— ·—— ·——· ·· — ··· · —·· · ·——· ·—
·— ·—· ·· ·—— · · ·—· — — · ·—— —— ·—·—·· ·—— · ·
·· —·· ·— —· —·—· —— ·——· · —·· —— ··· —·—·

·— ————— ·——· · ·—·—·· · ·——· ·— —· ·—— — ·· ·—·· ·—
·—· ·· · ·—— · · ·—· —— ··· ·—· ·—· —· · · ·· ·—
—— ·· · ·——· —— ··· —·—· ·—— ·—· ·—— ·—· —— ·—·—·· ·—
·—· ·· ·—·—·· —— · — ·—— ·—— ·—·—·· ·—· ··· ·—·—·· ·
·—·—·· ·· ·—— · · ·—· —— ··· —·—· ·—— · ·—·—·· ·—·—·
·—· ·· · —·—· · · ·—· —— ·—·—·· ·——· —— ·—·—·· ·—·—·
·—— ·—·—·· —· ···

···· ·—— —· —· · ·—· —·—· ·—— · · —·—· ·——· —— —· ·—
·—· ·· ·—— · ··· · ·—·—·· — —— —·—· ·—·—·· —·—· · ·
·—· ·· ·—·—·· ·——· · —· ·——· —·—· · · ·—·—·· ·—— · ·
·—· ·· · —·—· ·—— — ·—· ·—· ·——· · ·——· ·—·—·· ·——·
·—· ·· ·—·—·· —— ·—·—·· —— · ·—·—·· · · —— · ·—·—·
·—· ·· —— · ·——· · ·—· ·—·—·· —·—· ·—·—·· ·——· · —·
·—· · ·—·—·· ··· ·—·—·· ·—· ·—· —·—· ·—·—·· ·— · ·—·
·—·—·· —·—· —— ·——· —— · ·—·—·· ·—·—·· ·——· ·—·—·

— ·——·· ·—·—·· · · —·— · ·—— · · ·—· — ·—· ··· ————
·—— —·—· ·——· · ·—· ·—— ·—· ··· —— ·— ·—·—·· ·—· ————
·—· ·· —·—· ·—— · · —·—· ·—· · —·—· —— ·——· · ·——· ·—·
·— ·—· ·· —— · ·—·—·· ·—— ·—— —— · · ·—·—·· ·—·—·
·—· · · ·—· —·—· ·—— · ·· ·—· · —— ·——· · · ·—·—·
·—· ·· ·—· · —— · —·—· ·—— ·—·—·· · · ·——· · ·—·—·
·—— · ·—·—·· ·—— —— ·—·—·· ·——· —— · ·—·—·· ·—·—·
·· — ·—····

·— ·· —— ·—·—·· —— · · ·—— · —— · · · ·—— · · ·—
·—· ·· · — ·—— · · ·—· —— ··· ·—· —·—· ·—·—·· ·——· —·
·—· · · —·—· · · ·—· —— ··· —·—· ·—— · · —·—· · —·—·
·—· ·· —·—· —— · · —·—· ·—— ·—·—·· · · ·—·—·· —· ·
·—· · —— · —·—· · · —·—· ·—— ·—·—·· · · ·—·—·· ·—·—·
·—· · ·—·—·· —·—· · · —·—· ·—— ·—·—·· · ·—· · ·—·—·
·· · ·—· —— —·—· · — ·—· ·—·—·· —————— ————

SPECULATIVE FIELD STUDY

A warm summer twilight, a splinter of the serpentine lizard nature reserve.

The skies like bruised skin, blood leaking into the clouds.

Colour temperatures merging over time from red, through purple, to yellow, brown.

A confluence of converging boundaries.

The faint lunar glow of a diminishing sun of the earth's radiating light.

Crepuscular animal activities emerging during the twilight, both matutinal and vespertine.

A transitional drift that quickly gives way to the nocturnal behaviours.

Lucubrating over their symbiosis, the entangled planetary ecosystems of the overlooking satellites.

Sidereal and deep time compressed in sensors and ancient standing stones.

Faint fast moving smudges in the sky, bats swooping and darting in the aethereal spaces between windswept trees.

Moving so swiftly in the darkening skies, we
perceive a mere retinal after-vision of what's
happened.

Blurred impressions. Are they bats or the flashers
and floaters on the surface of my aging eye?

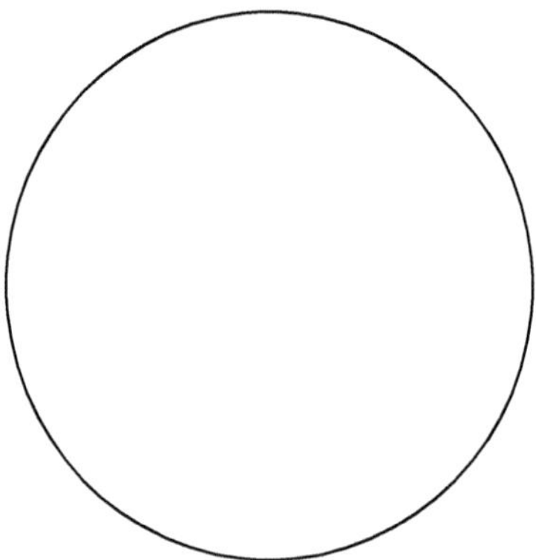

I reach for my echolocation sensor to amplify
its movements. However, I am too slow.

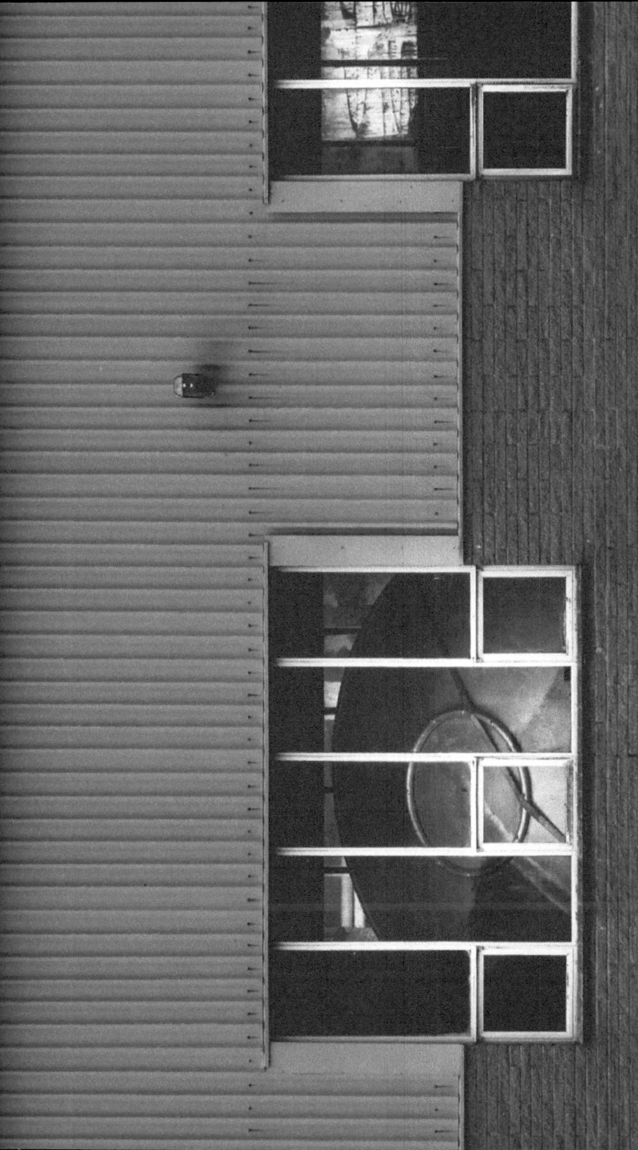

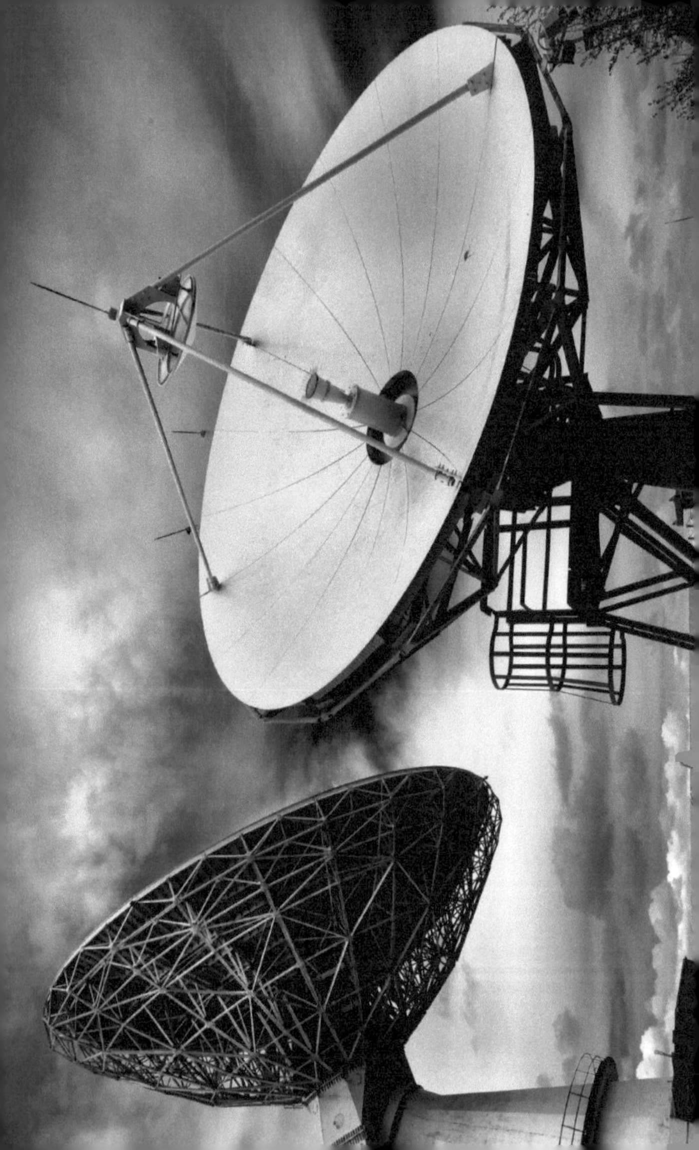

SUBTERRANEAN FIELD STUDY

Collecting mycelium ghosts.

Spectral branches hidden under rotting bark.

Subterranean shapes and forms,
just your fruiting bodies.

Acting in union and tension with others.

Collective engagement.

Continually responding, distributing nourishment
throughout the fungal body.

Multi-nodal, no beginning or end.

Rhizomorphic, tomentose and aerial,
complexities in flux.

Threads stretching miles, sending
and receiving information.

Chthonic cacophonic copulation, dissonances, resonances.

Saprophytic, feeding on dead organic material,
harmless and often beneficial.

Remedial powers, absorbing industrial toxins
from the soil.

You feed, die and cannibalise in the
nourishment of others.

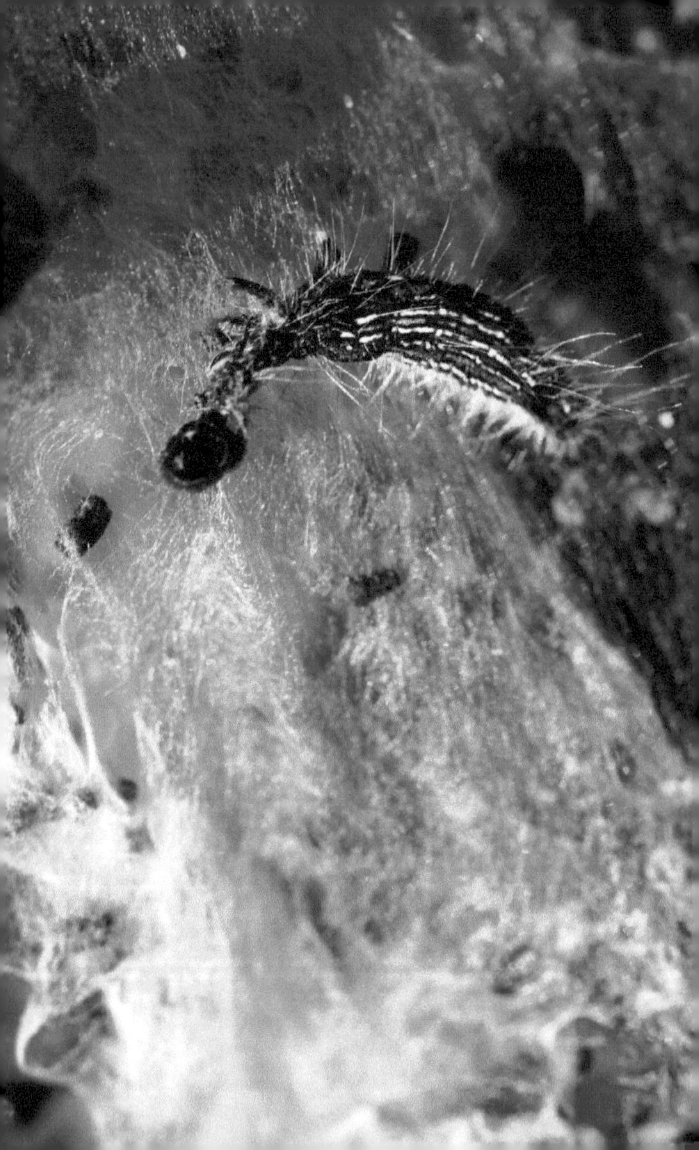

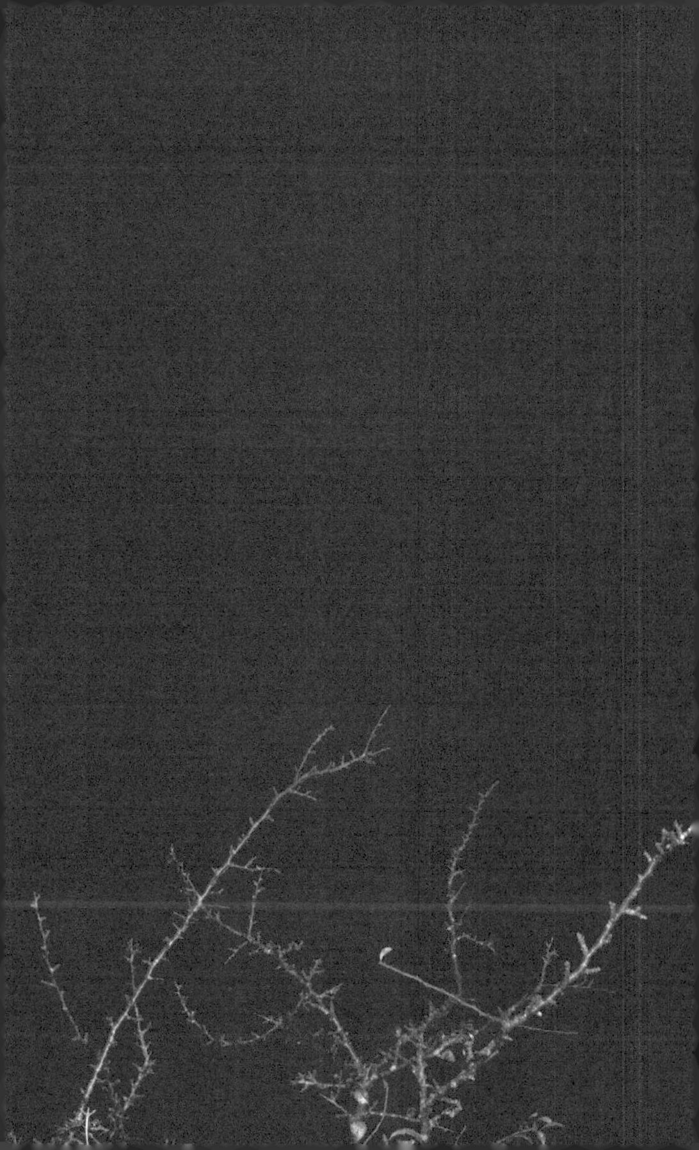

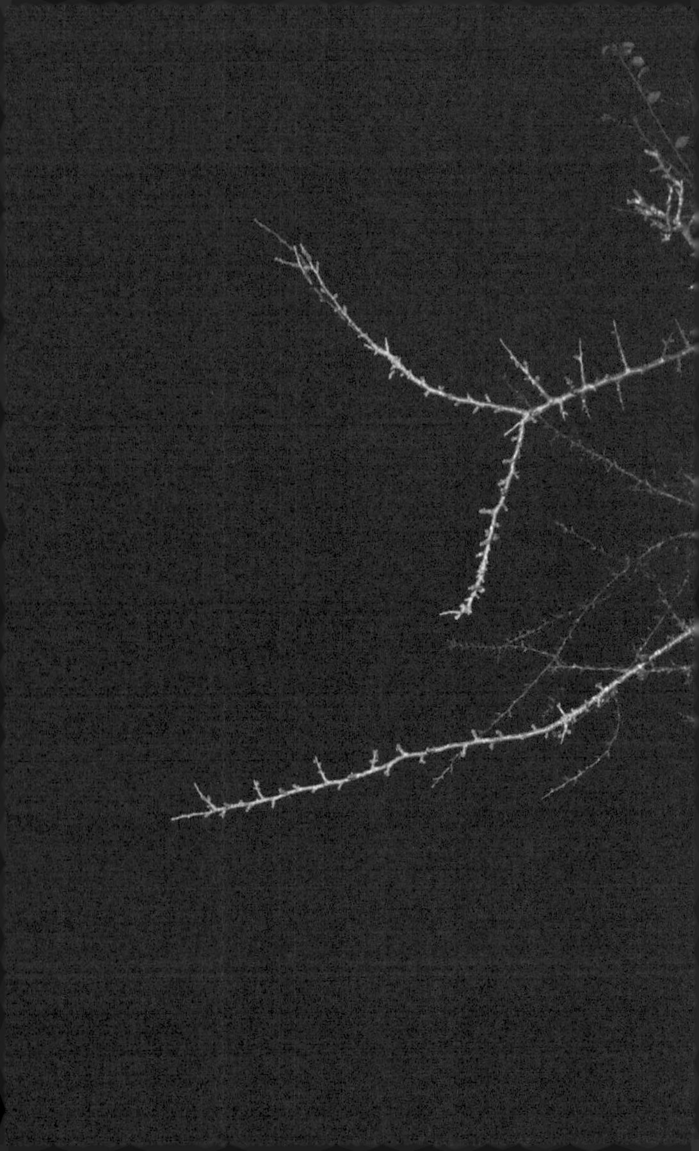

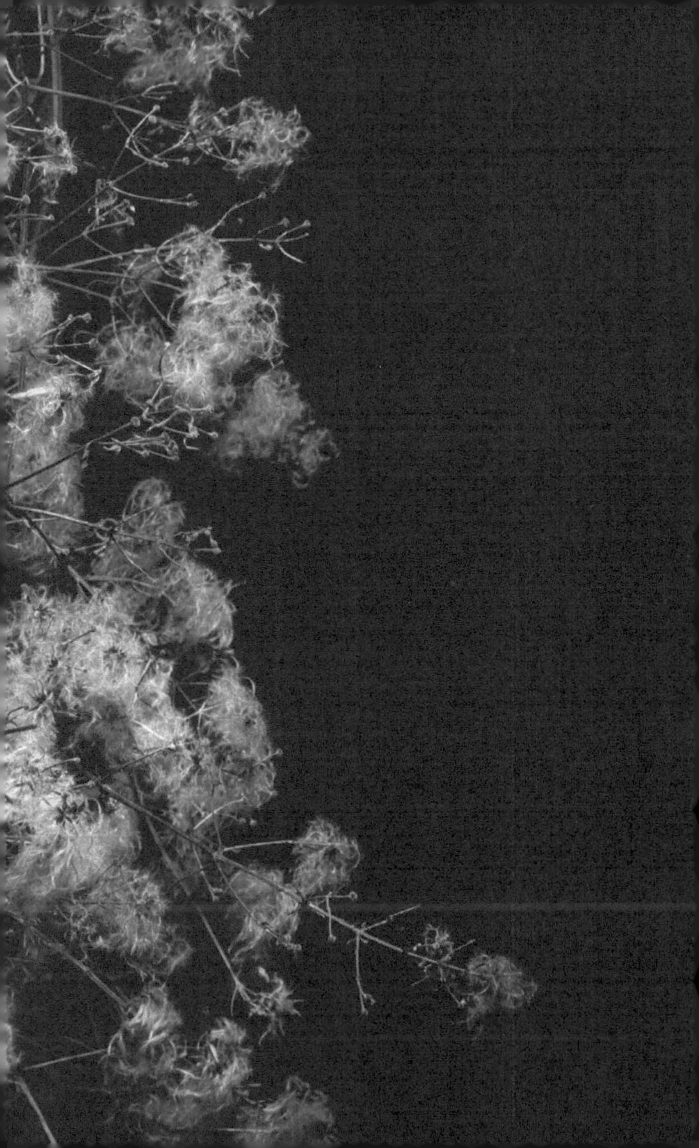

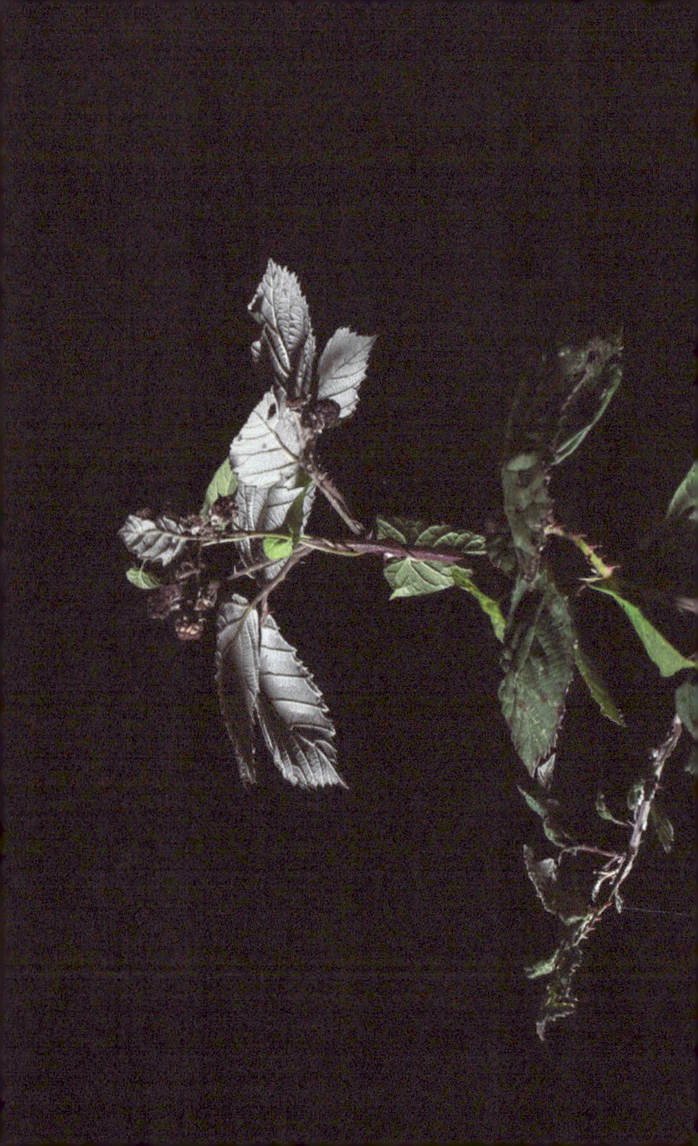

NOCTURNAL FIELD STUDY

AZMUTH ANGLE: 10 W
SATALLITTE: GHY-1

Travelling through the soil horizon.

Passing through thresholds of temperature.

Pockets of water and silt oozing and squelching.

Encountering unknown animal architectures.

Layers of minerals, humus and insects living,
dying, cannibalizing themselves, born again and
recycled.

Breaching the top soil boundary.

Plants that can possibly survive the acidic
conditions of the inhospitable moorland.

Dexter's, reds, or highland cattle wintered out
on the moors and folded at night.

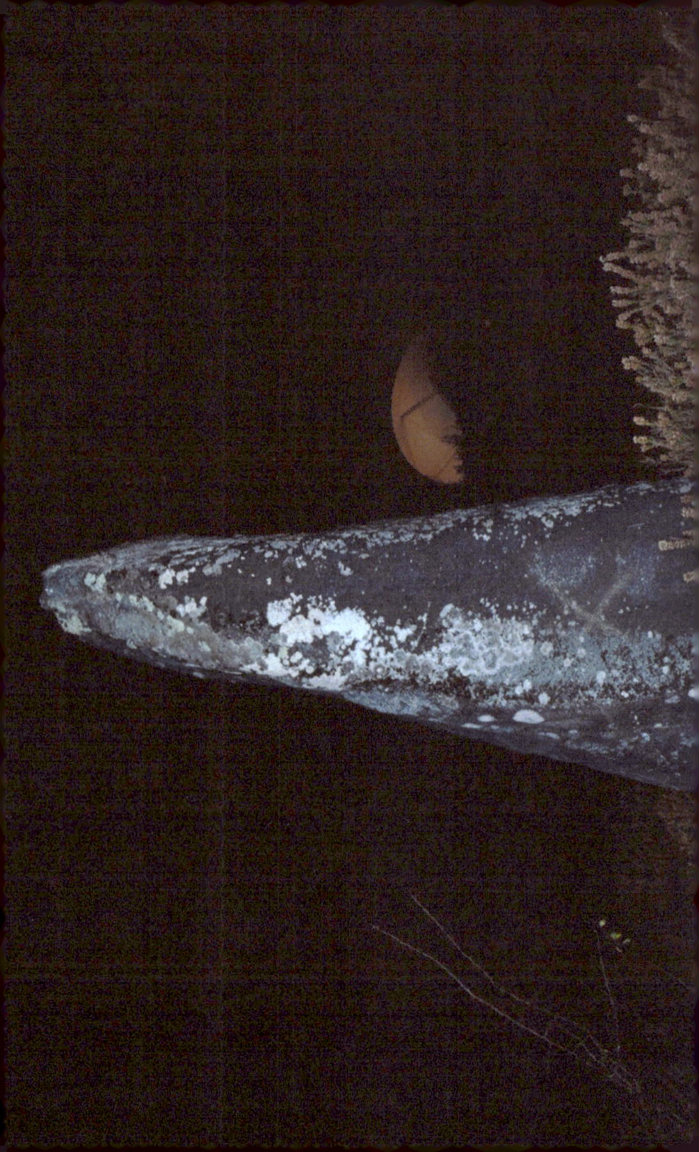

NOCTURNAL FIELD STUDY

AZIMUTH ANGLE: 30 W
SATELLITE: GHY-1

Plantarary thresholds of the unknown.

Fortifications riddled with concrete cancer.

Radar.

Sending.

Recovery.

Radio Squelch.

Hiss.

White noise.

Coded.

Signal jammed.

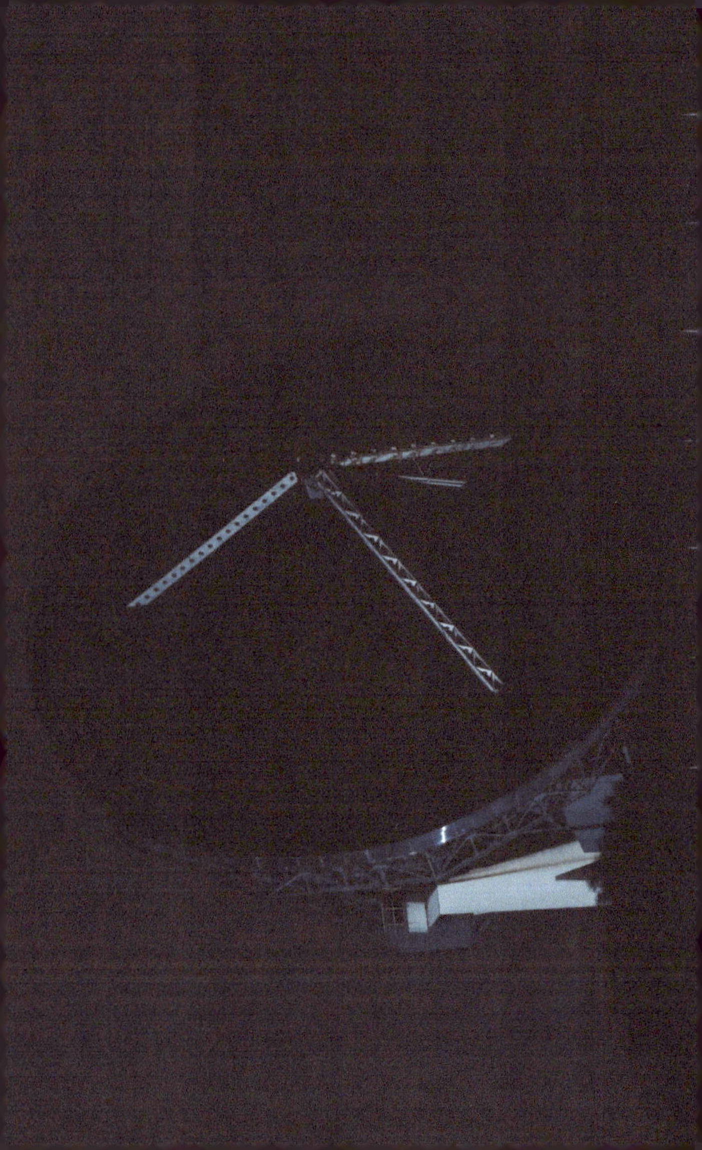

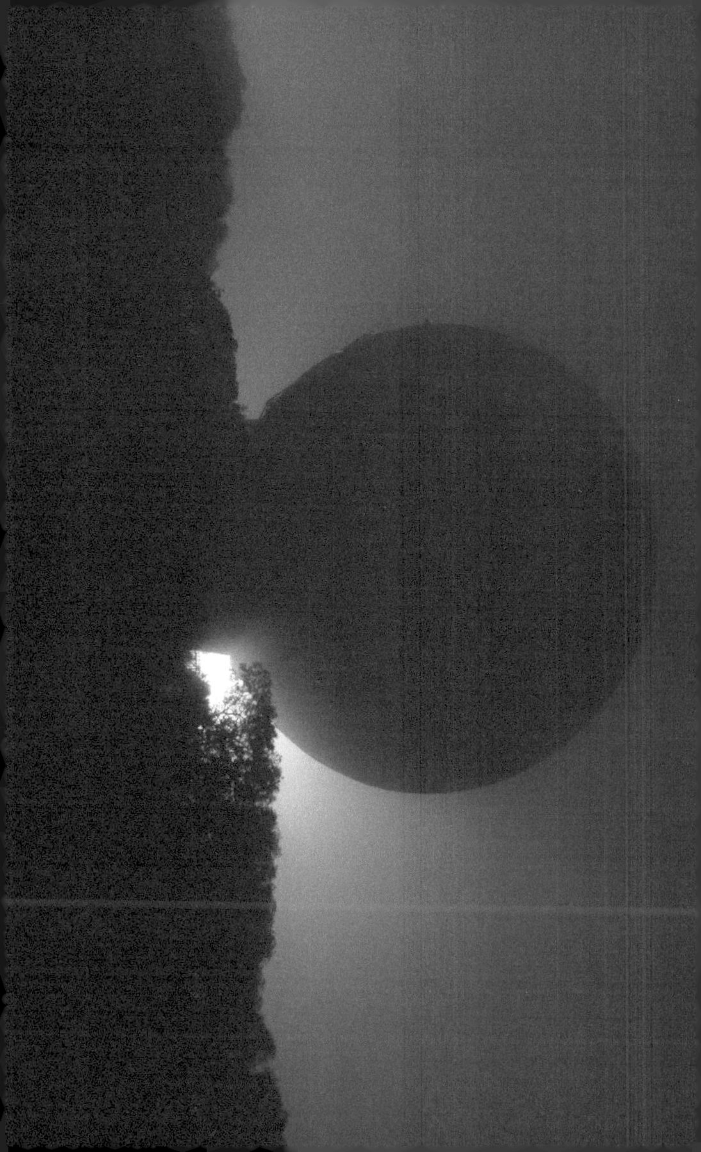

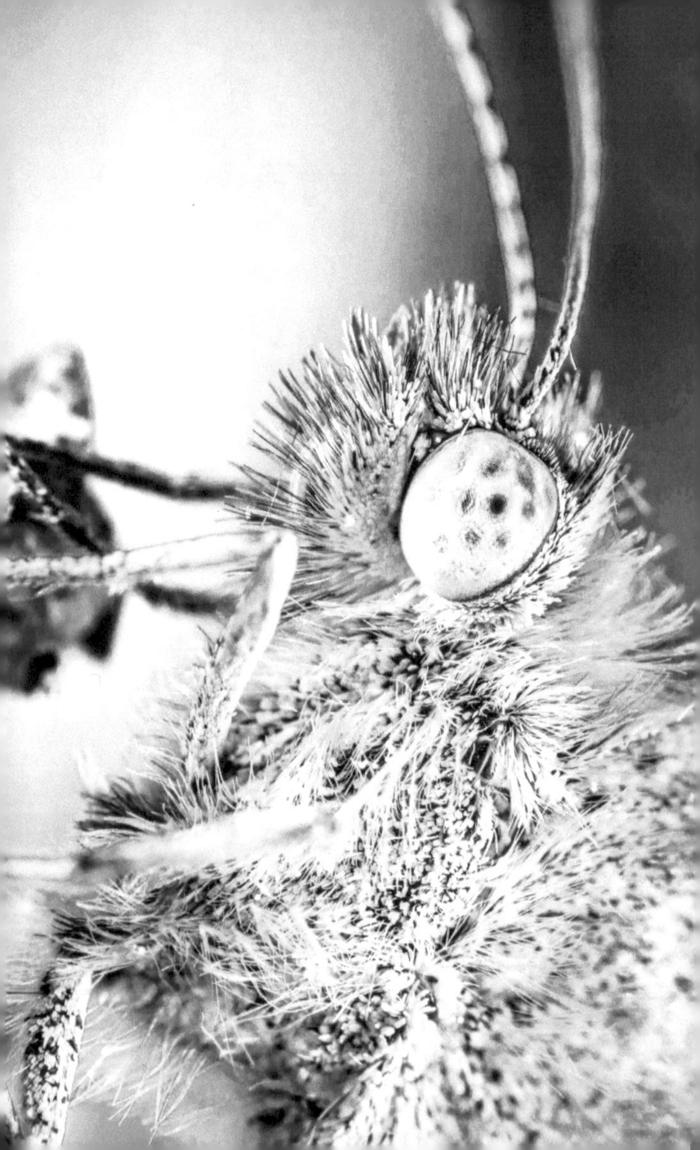

SONIC REFLECTIONS

Beneath the dense pollution of the anthropogenic airwaves, a wealth of tiny insects fill the air with barely audible high-pitched tones. Sparse atmospheres seething with intermittent bursts of activity.

I have spent long durations here; I am starting to understand what the sounds of the site mean.

Vast geological scales cast long contours across space and time, imposing a silent, tectonic indifference.

Deep earth time sounds unfold slowly to their own rhythms and timbres.

Rumbling subterranean vibrations, intensifying densities and distances.

The low hypnotic drone of wind farm propellers.

The creaking and grinding of the large satellites' mechanical gears, changing their Azmuth angles, moving in tune with the planet's slow deliberate movements. Where every slight shift could mean a transmission of millions of light years on other planets.

Satellite radiation can disrupt insects' navigation, communication, and reproduction by interfering with their reliance on natural electromagnetic signals.

The Downs' expansive undulating terrain is suffused with the murmur of matter transforming, expanding or disappearing, code-breaking signals, satellites transmitting and visualising unknown frequencies, ancient bridleways basking in intermittent sunlight. Wavering shadows of the Anthropocene and its many accumulating crises.

The Plantationocene

Capitalocene

Anthrobscene

Misanthropocene

Chthulucene

INDEX OF PLANTS AND SATELLITES

Viburnum Opulus
Goonhilly downs Cornwall UK
00:.00.
23/9/21
Azmuth Angle 64 W
GHY-3

Erica vagans
Goonhilly downs Cornwall UK
00.30
24/9/21
Azmuth Angle 64 W
GHY-3

Molinia caerulea
Goonhilly downs Cornwall UK
01:00
24/10/21
Azmuth Angle 64 W
GHY-3

Pyrus Mallus
Goonhilly downs Cornwall UK
01.15
24/10/21
Azmuth Angle 64 W
GHY-6

Pisonia aculeata L
Goonhilly downs Cornwall UK
22.00
7/11/21
Azmuth Angle 10 N
GHY-6

Prunus spinosa L
Goonhilly downs Cornwall UK
22.32
7/11/21
Azmuth Angle 10 N
GHY-3

Coprosma virescens Petrie
Goonhilly downs Cornwall UK
22.53
7/11/21
Azmuth Angle 10 N
GHY-3

Sparattanthelium uncigerum
Goonhilly downs Cornwall UK
23:05
7/11/21
Azmuth Angle 10 N
GHY-3

Pteridium aquilinum
Goonhilly downs Cornwall UK
00:30
21/11/21
Azmuth Angle 50 E
Antenna Farm

Nothofagus pumilio
Goonhilly downs Cornwall UK
00:46
21/11/21
Azmuth Angle 50 E
Antenna Farm

Deschampsia flexuosa
Goonhilly downs Cornwall UK
01.00
22/11/21
Azmuth Angle 50 E
Satallittes unknown (privately
owned)

INVENTORY OF ANTENNAS

GHY-3

Being equipped with a state-of-the-art super-cooled receiver means GHY-3 is ideally suited for use in SDA operations.

GHY-6

Deep Space mission's antenna supports Lunar and Deep Space mission operations.

ANTENNA FARM

GEO/MEO/LEO antennas for operators, broadcasters, and others to grow their businesses in near space.

NOTE

Goonhilly Earth Station provides TT&C, uplink/downlink services, and mission operations for spacecraft in LEO, MEO, GEO, and beyond.

Their portfolio of antennas currently focuses on S, C, X, Ku, and Ka band, with antenna sizes up to 32 m.

Jamie House combines art practice with photography and extended listening practices to enable non-anthropocentric readings of post-industrial sites. His experimental practice research methods include multi-sensory technological methods of observation, employing VHF, radio waves, Geiger counters, and textual responses.

Jamie is a multi-award-winning artist researcher. He has presented his work at International and National symposia and has exhibited and published widely.

www.jamiehouse.co.uk

CLOAK

Learn more at https://cloak.wtf